NEW E Wide Range Readers
BLUE BOOK 6

Fred J. Schonell
Phyllis Flowerdew

Oliver & Boyd

Acknowledgments

We are grateful to the following for supplying photographs and giving permission for their reproduction in this book:

BBC Hulton Picture Library, pp. 123, 144; The Bettmann Archive, Inc. and BBC Hulton Picture Library, p. 122; Camera 5, p. 77 (photo by Ken Regan); Bruce Coleman Ltd, pp. 53 (photo by Roger Wilmshurst), 136 (foot), 137 (top left)—photos by Jen and Des Bartlett, 137 (foot left—photo by Norman Tomalin); Colorsport, p. 75; Dor-O-Matic, p. 70; Eric and David Hosking, p. 101; Seaphot, pp. 135 (copyright Trevor E. Housby), 136 (top—photo by Christian Petron), 137 (top right—photo by Menuhin, foot right—photo by James H. H. Hudnall); Topham, p. 55.

Illustrated by Shirley Bellwood, Andrew Brownfoot, Tony Morris, R.A. Sherrington, Michael Strand and Pat Tourret. Cover illustration by Donald Harley.

Oliver & Boyd
Longman House
Burnt Mill
Harlow
Essex CM20 2JE

An Imprint of Longman Group UK Ltd-

First published 1950   Third edition 1976
Second edition 1965   Fourth edition 1985
Seventh impression 1992

© Phyllis Flowerdew and the Executors of the late Sir Fred J. Schonell 1965, 1985. (Except 'The Jumble Sale' © Anne B. English 1985 and 'The Champion' © Moira Miller 1985.)
All rights reserved. No part of this publication may be reproduced, stored in a retrieval system, or transmitted in any form or by any means, electronic, mechanical, photocopying, recording, or otherwise, without either the prior written permission of the Publishers or a licence permitting restricted copying issued by the Copyright Licensing Agency Ltd, 90 Tottenham Court Road, London W1P 9HE.

ISBN 0 05 003748 X

Set in Monophoto Plantin 12/16pt
Printed in Hong Kong
NMW/07

The Publisher's policy is to use paper manufactured from sustainable forests.

Preface

The Wide Range Readers are planned to provide graded reading practice for junior school children. Because children of 7–11 have a wide range of reading needs and attainments, there are three parallel series—Blue, Green and Red books—to provide plenty of material to suit the interests and reading ages of every child.

Books 1–4 are graded by half yearly reading ages, for use by appropriate groups within a class. Book 1 should provide an easy read for children with a reading age of about $7-7\frac{1}{2}$. Children with reading ages below 7 are recommended to use the Wide Range Starters.

The controlled vocabulary of the series makes the books suitable for the following reading ages:

$6\frac{1}{2}-7$	**Starter Books**—Blue, Green and Red
$7-7\frac{1}{2}$	**Book 1**—Blue, Green and Red
$7\frac{1}{2}-8$	**Book 2**—Blue, Green and Red
$8-8\frac{1}{2}$	**Book 3**—Blue, Green and Red
$8\frac{1}{2}-9$	**Book 4**—Blue, Green and Red
9+	**Book 5**—Blue, Green and Red
10+	**Book 6**—Blue, Green and Red
11+	**Book 7**—Red only
12+	**Book 8**—Red only

Contents

page
- 5 Friend from the Forest
- 14 The Wonderful Adventures of Baron Munchausen
- 20 The Boy who Loved Stars
- 30 Burst Pipes
- 33 The Jumble Sale
- 43 The Story of Soren Kanne
- 51 Extract from a Bird Diary
- 56 The Boy who Set the Birds Free
- 70 The Magic Doors
- 72 The Champion
- 79 The Run for Oklahoma
- 101 The Story of Flying
- 108 Helen in the Dark
- 124 Stories of Phineas Barnum
- 134 Did You Know This about Whales?
- 138 Radium

Friend from the Forest

Long ago in the forests of France a little deer lay sleeping in a glade. The sunshine and the dappled shadows played on her reddish coat, making it gleam like silk. She had fed well on grass and the young shoots that hid themselves among the roots of the trees. She had wandered down the forest paths, stopping a moment here and there—beauty in her slender body, grace in all her movements. Now she was sleeping, and there was nothing to disturb her except the sudden scamper of a playful squirrel in the tree-tops, or the quiet hum of some gauzy-winged insect flying past on an errand of its own. It was peaceful in the forest—peaceful and safe and beautiful, so the little deer sighed contentedly in her dreams, and slept the afternoon away.

Only when the later shadows fell across her silky coat, and the sunbeams danced away from the glade, only then did she waken. She opened her soft eyes, and slowly rose to her feet. She shook herself, and sniffed the cooling air. Then she walked away into the forest.

Usually when she walked, she went to the east, but today, for some reason, she went to the west. Slowly she walked, lifting her slim legs over spreading plants, or leaping high over tangled bushes. Soon she came to a small clearing, where her ears caught the sound of a stream bubbling over stones. Eagerly she went forward to find it. Then suddenly she stopped, and stood motionless within the shadows.

Before her was a rocky cave, and at the doorway of the cave sat a man. People meant danger! She must slip away before he saw her. But even as she stepped silently back into the shelter of the trees, she seemed to feel that there was something different about this man, and instead of running swiftly away, she stood still a little further back.

People meant danger! She had seen people once, long ago, and she still remembered the strange smell that had hung upon the air, and the loud, harsh sounds of human voices. She remembered that some men had come to the forest to kill and destroy, and she remembered the wild beating of her heart as she had sought to escape from them.

People meant danger. Yet there was something different about this man. He was dressed in a long, plain robe, and his feet were bare. As the deer watched, she saw a squirrel run up to him, and feed from his hand. She saw a bird fly down and perch upon his shoulder. These creatures had been as shy and timid as she herself—but they seemed to have no fear. It was almost as if this stranger could speak their language.

In curiosity the deer stepped a little nearer, and the man looked up and saw her. He smiled and stretched out a hand to welcome her. She took another step forward, and stopped again, uncertain what to do next.

"Come," said the man gently. "Come, little friend from the forest." The sound of his voice startled her, and she ran suddenly back among the trees.

It was several days before she went to the west again, and when she came once more to the clearing, the scene was much the same as it had been before. There was the man, standing by his cave, with birds and squirrels around him, and a friendly rabbit playing near. Again the little deer was curious, and her curiosity became even greater than her fear of humans, so that she stepped out into the open.

This time, when the man spoke to her, she did not run away, but went forward slowly.

She even let him stroke her with his outstretched hand, and she knew at once by his touch that though he was a human, he wanted her friendship and would never hurt her.

Once she had lost her shyness, the little deer went every day to the clearing in the forest. She would rub her head against the man's simple robe, and let him fondle her. She would sit on the grass beside him in the afternoon sun, and listen to his soothing voice. It became his habit to talk to her, and tell her his thoughts, and though she understood very little, she learned to love the musical sound of his gentle speech.

Bit by bit he told her all about himself, and how it was that he had come to the forest. His name was Brother Giles, and his home was in Athens, but one day he decided to leave his own country, and spend his life enjoying the beauties of nature, and giving thanks to God for them. So he sold all his possessions and wandered to the coast. When he reached it, a great storm was blowing, and out at sea a ship was tossing wildly up and down at the mercy of the wind and the waves. He knelt down on the beach and prayed that the ship would be kept safe. His prayer was quickly answered, for the storm died down almost at once and the ship sailed safely into port. As the ship had been saved by his prayers, he made up his mind to sail on her to whatever land she was going. So he had come to France, and here in the forest he had found the cave. Near by was the stream to refresh him, and there were herbs to serve as food, and birds and animals for friends.

So grew the friendship between Brother Giles and the little deer, and many were the hours they spent together in happiness and calm content.

* * * * * *

One morning the deer went out from her own home to look for food. She nibbled at tufts of fresh grass, and searched for the young, green shoots that hid themselves among the twisted roots of the trees. The sunshine and the dappled shadows played on her reddish coat so that it shone like silk.

Suddenly she heard a noise!

She lifted her head and listened. It was the sound of thudding hooves and barking dogs. It was the sound of blowing horns and the voices of men. Fear clutched at the little deer's heart. She stood quite still.

The sound came nearer. The horses, the men and the dogs were on her scent. They were hunting *her*—the little deer!

She leapt over a group of bushes, and ran as fast as she could, but even as she ran, she saw the king and his huntsmen close upon her. She saw the flash of scarlet and blue material, and the swing of velvet cloaks. She saw the galloping horses, and the dogs, mad with the excitement of the chase.

Through the trees, over the bushes went the deer, running like the wind, running with the swiftness of fear. Nearer and nearer came the huntsmen—horns blowing, dogs barking wildly.

On and on ran the deer, running in terror, running for her life! Somehow she managed to keep a little way ahead, travelling in a wide circle through the forest. But soon she grew tired, and her steps became shorter. She was burning with heat and panting with weariness.

Now the hunt was close behind her. In a moment the men would shoot with their bows and arrows, and the dogs would be upon her. Where could she run? Where could she hide?

Then she thought of Brother Giles. His cave was near. He was her friend. He would help her. If only she could reach Brother Giles, she would be safe. Hope gave her a moment of renewed strength. She turned sharply, surprising the huntsmen by her sudden change of direction. She plunged through the trees. She leapt over bushes, and she came out into the clearing where Brother Giles sat outside his cave.

If only she could get to him in time! Her silky coat was wet with heat, and her gentle eyes were wide with terror. At once Brother Giles saw what was happening.

"Come," he said softly. "Come, little friend."

The deer made one last effort, and rushed at Brother Giles.

"Shoot! Shoot!" cried the king at that moment, and through the air sped an arrow.

But the little deer was in Brother Giles' arms, and though she heard the sound of the arrow, she did not feel it strike her. Brother Giles must somehow have turned it away. She knew she was safe with Brother Giles.

Then the king and his huntsmen burst through the trees; and horses and dogs dashed madly into the clearing. But when the dogs reached Brother Giles and the deer, they drew back and their barking ceased. The horses stopped, and the huntsmen stared in amazement at the sight of a man protecting the hunted deer. In a single second all the excitement of the hunt had gone, all the fever of the chase was lost, and men and horses and dogs stood silent and ashamed. For there in the hand of Brother Giles, the hand that protected the little frightened deer, stuck an arrow! Brother Giles had been wounded to save his friend.

Only the sound of a bird song drifted from a treetop. Only the scamper of a squirrel was heard from the forest. In the clearing by the cave was silence—a breathless, breathless hush.

Then in shame and sorrow the king murmured,

"What have I done? What have I done?" And he fell to his knees, and clasped his hands.

"Forgive me, good and holy man," he begged. "I did not know that the deer was your friend."

"All animals are my friends," replied Brother Giles softly.

"And your poor hand," said the king anxiously. "The wound is deep. See how it bleeds. Return to the palace with me and stay until you are healed. Let me give you jewels and riches."

"No, no," answered Brother Giles. "Jewels and riches are not for me, and as for my hand, it will heal in time. What does a little pain matter, so long as my friend is safe?"

Sadly the king and the huntsmen mounted their horses, and rode back through the trees. The sound of trotting horses and pattering dogs died away and away in the distance, and the forest and Brother Giles and the little deer were left in peace once more.

* * * * * *

One day, long, long afterwards, a town was built in that very place, and the name it was given was Saint Giles. So people worked and slept, and children lived and laughed—where once Brother Giles had given thanks to God for the beauties of nature, and sunshine and dappled shadows had played on the reddish coat of the little deer.

The Wonderful Adventures of Baron Munchausen

Many, many years ago, in the days when people seldom travelled beyond their own villages, an unusual book was printed. It was called *The Travels of Baron Munchausen*, and it caused a great deal of talk and wonder. No one seemed to know anything about Baron Munchausen. Indeed some people thought it was just a name made up by someone who had probably never been on any travels at all. There was a picture in the front, of a soldier in a smart uniform. He had a long, curling moustache, a cut on his nose, and a patch on his cheek. He held a sword, and looked as if he might have fought dangerous battles in faraway places.

As for the story of his travels, it was most strange, and his adventures were simply wonderful—just a little bit *too* wonderful! Some of them are written here for you to read, but the Baron's grand sentences have been twisted round, and his long words have been left out, so that the wonderful adventures are easier to understand.

Lost in the Snow

One day in the middle of winter (*wrote Baron Munchausen*), I mounted my horse, and set off from Rome on a journey to Russia. The weather was bitterly cold, and the snow was so deep that in places I could not see the road at all.

On the way I passed a poor old man, dressed only in rags, and though I was cold myself, I was sorry for him, and I threw him my coat.

After a while darkness began to fall, and I looked for somewhere to spend the night. There was no village to be seen. There were no houses, no trees. As I did not know the road, I decided that I should have to sleep out of doors. In any case, the snow was so deep now that it was difficult for my horse to travel. I looked round for something to which I could fasten him, when I noticed what appeared to be a small, pointed stump of a tree sticking up in the snow. I tied the horse's bridle securely to it, put my pistols under my arm for safety, and lay down in the snow. I was so tired that in spite of my cold bed, I slept soundly all night.

When I awoke, I found it was daylight. To my surprise I saw the snow had all melted, and I was lying on the ground in a churchyard. Close by was a church, and beyond the gate were streets and houses.

"This is strange," I thought. "I saw no sign of a village here last night." I looked round for my horse, but he was not in sight. I knew he could not have wandered away, for his bridle was strong, and my knot could not possibly have come loose. I walked up and down the churchyard, and even out into the street, but I could not find him anywhere.

Suddenly I heard him neighing, but still I could not see him.

"This is most strange," I said aloud. "I can hear his voice, yet I cannot find him." Just then I happened to look upwards, and to my amazement, I saw my horse hanging by his bridle from the top of the church steeple!

For a moment I could not believe my own eyes. However had he managed to get up there, at the very top of the steeple?

Then I understood what had happened. The snow had been so deep the day before that it had covered the whole village. Streets, shops, houses, even the church had been buried. During the night the weather had changed, and the snow had thawed, so that I, while asleep, had sunk gently down to the churchyard as the snow had melted away. What I had thought to be a broken stump of a tree sticking up in the darkness had really been the point of the church steeple, and it was there that I had fixed the bridle of my unfortunate horse.

Now of course I had to get him down again, but it took me only a second to think how to do that. I pointed one of my pistols at the church steeple, and shot the bridle in two. Down came my horse.

So I was able to continue my journey into Russia.

A Narrow Escape

One day I was travelling through the forests of Poland, when a fierce and terrible wolf rushed suddenly upon me. At that time I had neither sword nor pistol. There was not even a stick with which I could defend myself.

I had no time to think of a plan, and as the wolf sprang upon me, I thrust my fist into his open mouth. I pushed so hard that my arm went into his body, right up to my shoulder!

Now what was I to do? If I pulled out my arm, the wolf would fly at me more angrily than before. If I did not pull it out, my position would be just as difficult.

For a moment I stood facing those flaming eyes. Then quickly I took hold of the wolf's tail, and turned him inside out like a glove. I flung him to the ground, left him there, and continued my journey.

A Traffic Problem

One bitterly cold winter my driver and I were travelling through Russia in a carriage, when we came to a narrow lane. Knowing that it was wide enough to take only one carriage, I feared that some other travellers might appear suddenly round the bend, and bar our way.

"Blow your horn!" I shouted to the driver. "Blow your horn, to give warning of our approach."

The driver put the horn to his lips to blow a merry tune, but no sound came. He tried again, blowing and blowing with all his might, but he could not make the horn give a single note. Just as we were wondering what was wrong with it, we suddenly saw another carriage coming towards us. Fortunately both drivers stopped in time to avoid an accident—but of course it was impossible for the carriages to pass.

However, I am fairly strong, so I climbed out of my carriage, lifted it, wheels and all, above my head, and jumped with it over a high hedge into a field. Then I gave another jump over the hedge, and landed back in the road again, just past the other carriage. I then returned for the two horses, lifting one up on my head, and holding the other under my arm. I managed the first jump fairly easily, but before I could make the second, the horse under my arm began to kick and snort. I slipped his back hooves into my coat pocket, and jumped back into the lane.

So the other carriage was passed in safety, and my driver and I continued our journey.

Soon we arrived at an inn, where we decided to stay the night. We were glad indeed to find good food and a blazing fire. The driver hung his horn on a peg near the fireplace, and we sat down to warm ourselves. Suddenly we heard music. It seemed to come from our own horn, though no one was blowing it!

Then we knew why the driver had been unable to play it in the lane. His tunes had frozen inside the horn, and now the warmth of the fire was thawing them. So we sat there for some time, listening to one tune after another until all the frozen music had been played.

At the end of his adventure the Baron wrote—"Some travellers tell stories which are not always quite true. I am always very careful to keep to the truth. Now I will tell you more of my adventures, and I assure you that they are as true as those I have already told."

What do *you* think about the wonderful adventures of Baron Munchausen?

The Boy who Loved Stars

Tycho Brahe sat by the window, and gazed out into the darkness. The wind sighed in the trees, and the moon threw long dark shadows across the smooth, silver lawns. It was a beautiful night. The garden looked unreal and lovely, like a garden in a dream; and the stars twinkled in the sky like candles flickering against a velvet curtain. Stars! Stars! How Tycho loved them! How they fascinated him, with their patterns and their changing positions. How wonderful they were—so bright and steadfast, so strange and mysterious.

Tycho pushed the window open a little wider, moving it very carefully so that it should not creak and disturb anyone in the house. It is a lonely feeling to be awake when everyone else is asleep, but Tycho did not mind as long as the stars were shining. Tonight he had a special reason for being restless and wakeful. He was thinking about the morning, for then he was going on a long journey to a new school in a different part of Denmark.

"I wish I didn't have to go," he murmured to himself. "I wish I could stay here."

He felt unhappy at the thought of leaving his uncle, and his friends, the woods and the lanes, and all the things he knew.

A star gave an extra twinkle. It seemed to shine right

down on his face, to comfort him.

"Anyway," he thought, "I'll still have the stars. They'll be the same—the Pole Star, the Plough and the Milky Way—all the patterns that I know. I'll still have those for company."

He crept back into bed, and lay with his eyes wide open. He hoped he would like the school. His uncle, who was very rich, wanted him to work hard, and to study law and government so that when he grew older he would be able to help in the ruling of the country.

Tycho of course was more interested in the sun and the moon and the stars, and he wondered if there would be any lessons on things like that. Oh well, as long as there was a window at school, through which he could gaze at night, he would be happy. His thoughts wandered again to the stars that he loved, and thinking of them, he fell asleep.

Tycho's life had begun in an unusual way. His father, whose name was Otto, and his Uncle George were brothers. Uncle George had no children, and his greatest wish was for a son, so at the time of Otto's marriage, they made a strange bargain with each other. Otto and his wife agreed that they would give their first baby boy to George. They intended to keep their promise, but when Tycho their child was born, they felt very differently about it.

George soon arrived at the house to claim the child.

"No," said Otto. "We want him ourselves."

"But you promised," replied George.

"It was all very well to promise while I had no child," protested Otto, "but now I've changed my mind. He's my son, and I refuse to give him up to you."

George was angry and disappointed. Sadly he went back to his large house and his servants. All his money, and no one on whom to spend it! All these riches and no one to inherit them!

About a year later a second son was born to Otto.

"Now," thought George, "I'll see that the bargain is kept," and he visited his brother's house in secret, and stole away the first child. So it was that Tycho came to live with Uncle George. And now he was nearly thirteen years old, and going away to a boarding school.

★ ★ ★ ★ ★ ★

The thing that Tycho remembered most about his first year at school was nothing to do with lessons and games, or boys and masters. It was to do with the sun. It was an eclipse. People said that on a certain day the shadow of the moon would cover part of the sun. "How does anyone know?" asked Tycho, and he half expected that nothing would happen at all, but it did.

On that day in the year fifteen hundred and sixty, a shadow crept over the edge of the sun. Breathless with excitement, Tycho watched it. Slowly, slowly it moved across the face of the sun—a black circle upon a golden one—covering part of the brightness, hiding part of the light.

Tycho's heart beat fast. This was so strange, so mysterious.

Then the shadow became smaller and smaller, and slipped away till the sun was full and clear again, shining in splendour.

An eclipse! How wonderful it was! But the most

wonderful thing about it was that people had known that it would happen. They had known the year, the day, and even the time—just as they knew when the stars would change their positions in the sky! How did they know these things?

"There must be books," thought Tycho.

In those days books were scarce, and difficult to obtain, especially the kind that Tycho needed, but after a while he managed to obtain one. It explained the movements of the sun and the moon and the stars, but alas, it was not written in Danish, the language he spoke, but in Latin.

"Oh, well," said he, "I'll have to work a bit harder at Latin so that I can understand it."

So the boy astronomer worked and studied, and watched the stars; and he dreamed of the day when he would make his own instruments for measuring distances, and have his own house, with great windows looking out across the skies—a temple built for the study of stars. Then he would spend his whole life solving their mysteries.

Uncle George meanwhile was not so pleased. He wanted Tycho to learn about law and government; and according to the reports from school, he was spending nearly all his days reading about stars, and half his nights gazing at them.

"It's all a waste of time," declared Uncle George angrily one holiday.

"But it's so interesting," answered Tycho.

"Interesting!" exclaimed Uncle George. "It's a waste of time. How will stars help you to make laws for the country? How will knowledge of eclipses help you to govern Denmark?"

Tycho was now sent to Germany, where his uncle hoped he might forget about stars, and give his attention to more useful subjects. To make sure of this, a tutor named Vedel was sent too, with instructions to see that Tycho studied law.

Poor Vedel! His task was quite hopeless. Every time Vedel went out of the room, Tycho took out the small globe which he kept hidden, and from it he learnt the names of stars. The law books stood on the shelves unread, and Tycho spent his money on books of astronomy. He made wooden instruments (this was before the days of telescopes) and when Vedel was asleep at night, Tycho crept out in the darkness, and measured the distances between stars.

At last Vedel knew that he would never be able to make this boy learn about law and government, so he gave up trying, and the two then became firm friends.

Thus Tycho Brahe grew up, interested only in stars, stars, stars.

* * * * * *

One night, after a hard day's work, Tycho was walking home to supper with some servants when he happened to glance up at the group of stars known as Cassiopeia. There it was, so easy to find—like a great W in the sky—the same as ever.

But it was not the same! It was different. Tycho stood

still and stared, hardly able to believe his eyes. There in Cassiopeia was a new star—clear and shining, dazzling and brilliant!

"I'm dreaming," thought Tycho. But no—there he was on the stony path. There was his house in front, and there were his servants beside him. But in the sky was a new star, unexpected, unknown!

"I'm imagining it," thought Tycho.

Yes, that must be what was happening. He was imagining it.

The servants stood talking quietly, waiting for their master.

"Look!" cried Tycho in excitement. "Look at Cassiopeia. How many stars do you see there in that great W?"

The servants looked up at the sky. Would they say

five, the usual number, the number that had always been there before?

"Six," said one.

"That's right," said the others. "Six."

"Then it's true, it's true!" cried Tycho. "I've discovered a new star. Oh, how beautiful! How beautiful!" And Tycho Brahe stood gazing at the brilliance of that twinkling light, and he was lost in the wonder of a new star.

After that, his name spread through Europe, and he was given honours and fame. But still he dreamed of a special house in some quiet place—a temple built for the study of stars.

Then one day his dream came true. He was living in Germany, where he now had a wife and children of his own, when early one morning a messenger arrived, summoning him to the palace of the King of Denmark. What did the king wish to say, Tycho wondered, as he travelled day and night back to his own country. He was soon to know.

"You are the greatest astronomer in Europe," said the King. "What is your dearest wish?"

"Your Majesty," replied Tycho, "I should like a quiet place where I can live with my family, undisturbed, and watch the heavens. I should like a temple where I can study the stars."

Then the King gave him a little island near the coast

of Denmark. He gave him money and instruments, and a house and gardens. He gave him the greatest temple that had ever been built for the study of stars.

And there Tycho Brahe lived and studied in peace, with the waves washing round the shores of his island home, and the moon sending beams of light across the silvery lawns. There at night he watched the patterns and the changing positions of the stars.

Stars! Stars! How wonderful they were—so bright and steadfast, so strange and mysterious.

Burst Pipes

Jack and Joan were alone in the house. Snow had been falling for several days, and the weather was so cold that they were glad to stay by the fire and read. Father was at work, and Mother was out shopping. Everything was very quiet.

Then came a small sound,

"Drip, drip, drip."

"What's that?" asked Jack, looking up.

"I can't hear anything," murmured Joan, without raising her eyes from her book.

Jack was too warm and comfortable to get up and look, so he went on reading.

"Drip, drip, drip." It was louder now.

"Something's dripping," said Jack. "Someone must have left the tap running." This time he went upstairs to see.

To his surprise there was a pool of water on the landing. It was coming from beneath the bathroom door, and the dripping sound was now very loud indeed.

Jack opened the bathroom door. Whatever was happening? The floor was flooded, and water was falling from the ceiling like rain. Jack gave a shout that brought Joan running up the stairs.

"The pipes must have burst," said Jack.

"What'll we do?" said Joan.

For a few moments they both stood and stared. "Better find Mother," said Jack at last.

Hurriedly they put on coats and rushed round to the shops. It was quite a while before they found their mother, and by the time they all reached home again, the bathroom ceiling was damaged, water was flooding the landing and rushing down the stairs, and the carpets were ruined.

Jack and Joan might have saved their mother and father a lot of expense and worry if they had only known what to do when the pipes burst!

If a pipe burst in your house when you were alone, would *you* know what to do?

In the winter when there is frost and snow, the water in the pipes leading from the tank to the taps gets colder and colder until it freezes and turns to ice. Ice takes up more room than water, and sometimes it hasn't enough space in which to expand, so it bursts the pipe. Later the house gets a little warmer. The ice melts and turns back to water. Then the water drips through the ceiling and pours down the walls.

You must do something quickly, before your house is spoiled! There are three things to do.

The first, and most important, is to turn off the water at the main so that no more will flow through the pipes to the storage tank.

The second is to turn on all the taps in the house so

that any water left in the pipes will run into the bath and basins, and not through the floor.

The third is to fetch a plumber to mend the burst.

It's all quite easy, isn't it? But even if Jack and Joan had known the three things to do, I am sure they wouldn't have known where to find the main.

Do you know where to find yours? It might be:

1. On the front of a pipe under the kitchen sink or on a pipe against a wall.

2. In the larder or in a cupboard.

3. Out of doors, hidden under a little iron lid in the ground, in the garden or even in the street. A plumber may have to turn it off with the long iron key known as a turnkey, so find out where the turnkey is kept too.

So remember, if your pipes burst, *turn off the water at the main.*

Find the main today. Find it before the weather gets colder, the frosts come, the water freezes and turns to ice, and the pipes burst!

The Jumble Sale

Jim and Ali stood at the door of the youth club. They looked glum.

"How can we play table tennis without a table?" said Jim. His dad had just told him that the old table couldn't be mended. "I'm sorry Jim, but the wooden frame is rotten. I can't patch it up any more," he said.

Ali kicked at the stones on the path. "If we can't practise, we have no chance of winning the tournament."

The table tennis tournament was still two months away, but Jim knew that Ali was right. There were some very good players in the district. Jim and Ali had never won the title, although they had reached the quarter-finals. If they couldn't practise for their doubles match, they'd be beaten in the first round.

Shirley and Mary walked across the muddy stretch of grass to join the boys.

"Your dad has just told me about the old table," Mary said to Jim. "What are you going to do?"

Jim shook his head. "What can we do? We need a proper table, or we'll have no chance in the tournament."

They stood outside the door, watching the other youth club members coming and going. It was a busy and popular club, and they were the most senior members. A lot of the younger ones enjoyed playing table tennis too. They were talking about starting a junior team.

"It's up to us to do something," Mary said, after a silence. "Why don't we advertise for a second-hand table? Somebody must have a table they don't want."

But Jim said that was no use. A second-hand table would cost money, and they had none.

Cliff, the leader of the youth club, had already held a sponsored walk to raise money for new table tennis bats. These were locked inside the games cupboard, but now there was no table to play on.

It was Shirley who had the bright idea. They would raise the money themselves.

"Let's have a jumble sale," she suggested. "It's a long time since we held one in the club."

She looked round at the long streets of houses stretching away in every direction. If they called at all those houses and explained what the jumble sale was for, surely people would give them things to sell. It was for a good cause.

They went indoors to discuss the idea with Cliff.

"It's worth a try," he told them. "We certainly can't afford to buy a table, even a second-hand one. Go ahead, but don't expect too much."

Soon a date was fixed, and they all had jobs to do. Mary, who had neat handwriting, wrote the notices advertising the jumble sale. Shirley, Jim and Ali went round the local shops and asked if they would display the notices in the windows. Ali's parents said they would put one on their van as well as in their shop window.

The next afternoon they set out to collect for the jumble sale. Shirley's mum lent them the baby's pram. It was an old pram, but they still had to be careful with it. "Don't pile heavy things on it," she called after them, as they wheeled the pram away.

"No, Mum! Of course we won't," said Shirley. "Ali's dad says he'll collect the heavy stuff in his van."

None of them enjoyed collecting the jumble. It was hard work pushing the pram up and down the long streets, knocking on doors and explaining about the jumble sale.

"We're collecting for a jumble sale at the youth club. It's to raise money for a table tennis table. The old one is broken and can't be mended. Please, have you any jumble you can give us?"

Over and over again they said the same words. At some houses they were given nothing, but at others they were luckier. By the end of the afternoon the pram was piled high with bundles of clothes, piles of odd dishes, and a few ornaments and paperback books. One man gave them a giant teddy bear. He'd won it in a raffle, but he didn't really want it.

Jim sat the teddy bear on top of the jumble and Shirley pushed the pram back to the youth club.

Cliff was waiting for them. He wanted them to unpack the jumble from the pram before they went home.

"The china can go in these cardboard boxes, and then you'd better sort through the bundles of clothes." he told them.

They all groaned. "Can't we just dump them and go home?" asked Shirley. "My feet ache."

Cliff shook his head. "It's better to know what's inside the bundles."

He began lifting the bundles out of the pram and

spreading them on the long trestle table. "Come on, think of the money for a new table."

They worked in silence, sorting the clothes into different sizes. Shirley found a large hat with flowers on the brim. She stuck it on her head and pranced down the room, making them laugh. Then Jim held up a waterproof jacket.

"Look at this. It's scarcely been worn. I wouldn't mind buying it myself." He put it on and fastened the zip. "It fits me, too."

They had nearly finished now. Jim unrolled the final bundle. Inside were two shrunken pullovers and an old-fashioned blue waistcoat.

Cliff smiled when he saw the waistcoat.

"It's a long time since I saw one of those. My grandfather always wore one with his Sunday best suit. See this small pocket? He kept his pocket watch in there." Cliff ran a finger round inside the pocket. "There's something in here," he said excitedly, and he pulled out—one old penny. Everyone laughed.

"It's my lucky day! One old penny," he grinned.

"We can't even add it to the table tennis fund," Mary said. She took the coin from Cliff and rubbed it on her sleeve. "It's quite shiny and new looking, even though it is old."

Ali asked how old it was. Mary peered at the coin in her hand.

"The date is 1902. You can read it easily. And the head on the other side is of Edward VII."

Jim asked if he could take the penny home and show it to his brother.

"He collects old coins," Jim explained. If he hasn't a 1902 penny, he might be interested in this one."

The next day, as Cliff was unlocking the doors of the youth club, Jim came rushing up. He held out the old penny, and Cliff took it back. "Doesn't your brother want it?" he asked.

"He wants it," Jim beamed at the others as they arrived. "He wants it. The trouble is, he can't afford it." Pulling a booklet from his pocket he said,

"Here's the entry in the coin collectors' book. It's an

Edward VII penny, dated 1902, and as good as new. It's a rare coin, Cliff, and it's valuable. What shall we do now?"

What they had to do first, was to find out who the coin belonged to. That meant going round all the houses again, carrying the rolled up bundle of waistcoat and pullovers. They asked at every house, until they found the old man who had given it to them. Then Cliff had to explain about the penny they had found in the waistcoat pocket.

"There are shops in the town that buy old coins," Cliff told him. "You could sell it, unless you want to keep it."

But the old man thought he would rather sell it. He couldn't believe that the coin was worth so much.

"It's only a penny, after all," he said. "Thank you all for giving it back to me."

There was now a lot of work to be done. All the goods had to be priced and set out on the tables in the club.

Then when at last the jumble sale was over, Cliff counted the money.

"You've done quite well," he said. "But we do really need a little more. You'll have to think of a way of raising a bit more money."

The four of them groaned at the very thought of more fund raising.

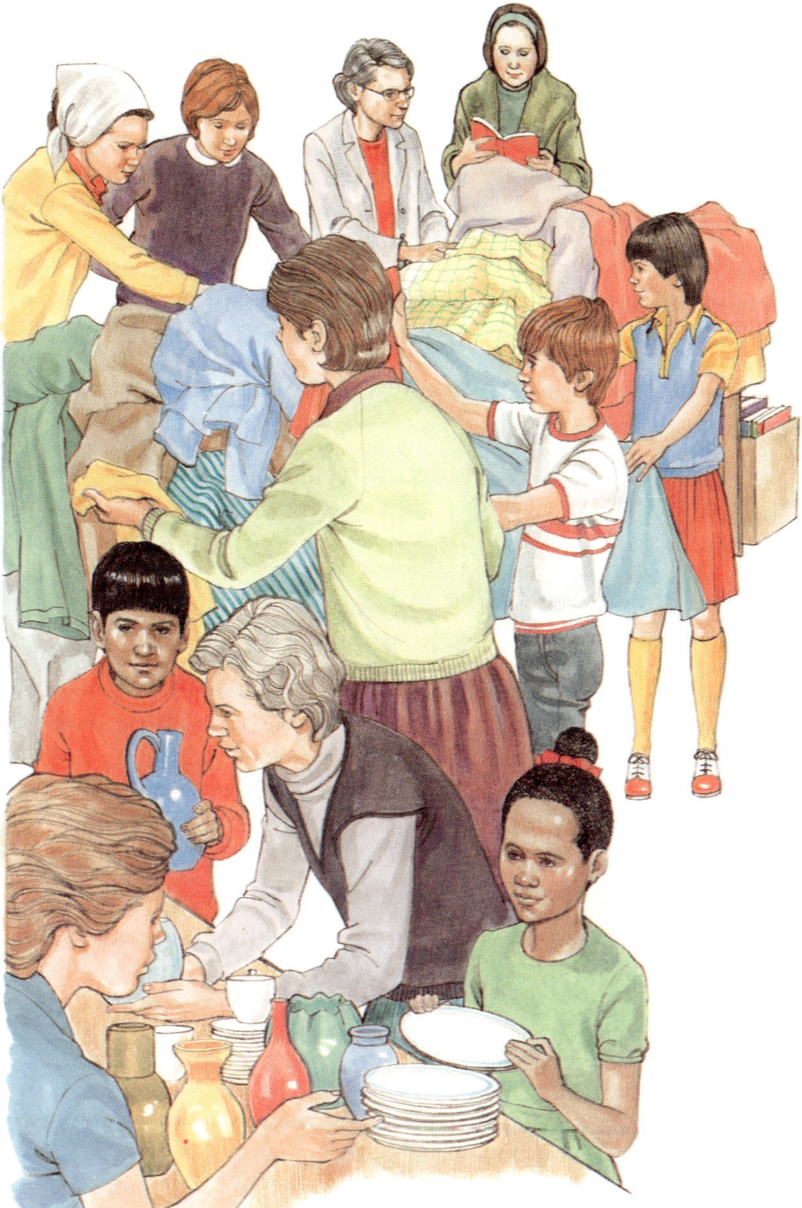

Then two days later, Cliff came into the club waving an envelope.

"Jim, Ali, Shirley, Mary," he called. "This is our lucky day. Guess what's in the envelope?" He couldn't wait to tell them. "There's money in here. Lovely crinkly money!"

The old man had sold his 1902 penny for more than he'd expected and he hadn't forgotten them. He had given Cliff some of the money to spend on the youth club.

"It's yours." Cliff handed it to them. "Add it to the jumble sale money."

"Now we can afford a good, strong table," said Shirley, her eyes shining.

Jim and Ali faced each other across an imaginary table, hitting invisible balls backwards and forwards between them. Faster and faster they went, yelling with delight, until they flopped on the floor, completely out of breath.

"Come on, all of you," laughed Mary. "Let's go out and look for a good second-hand table. These two need to practise if they're ever going to be the champions."

"At least we've got a chance now," Jim said. "Come on, let's go."

Anne B. English

The Story of Soren Kanne

Long ago, as the sun was setting over Denmark, a little boat sailed out to sea. The master of the ship trimmed the sails so that they caught the evening breeze, but the boy who was with him sat for a moment, looking at the shore. Beyond the sand dunes that rose like small, yellow hills on the beach, he saw green fields and spreading forests. He watched the shadows deepening, until all the land was as grey as the sea. Then he hung up a lantern at the front of the ship, and remarked,

"It's calm tonight. It will be good for fishing, won't it?"

"I'm not so sure," replied the sailor. "It seems *too* calm to me."

They sailed along in silence for a while, and the night became very dark. Land merged into sky, and sky into sea. Only the lantern swayed in the blackness, making a pool of yellow light on the fluttering sail, and a small path of silver on the sea. There was no sound except the sigh of the breeze and the wash of the water round the ship. The ship's master puffed at his pipe.

"I'm going back. The water is too calm. I don't trust it," he said slowly.

"Oh," said the boy in disappointment. "It's such a good night for fishing."

The man shook his head, and suddenly, even before he had time to change his course, a great wind arose as if from nowhere. It blew the waves against the little ship, and sent it tossing helplessly high and low. It tore at the sails, and shrieked around the mast as though it would snap it in two.

The boy rose unsteadily to his feet, and did his best to help the man to turn the boat, but now the storm broke about them in full force. Rain beat wildly in their faces. Thunder roared overhead, and vivid flashes of lightning lit up the sky. The waves rose higher and higher, towering above the boat and crashing down upon it in fury. The sailor and the boy both knew that nothing they could do now would get the boat back into harbour. They would just have to keep it afloat till the storm died down, and hope that they would be kept safe till then.

Meanwhile the little sailing boat was driven farther and farther from its course, and swept on round the coast of Denmark. All night long the man and the boy

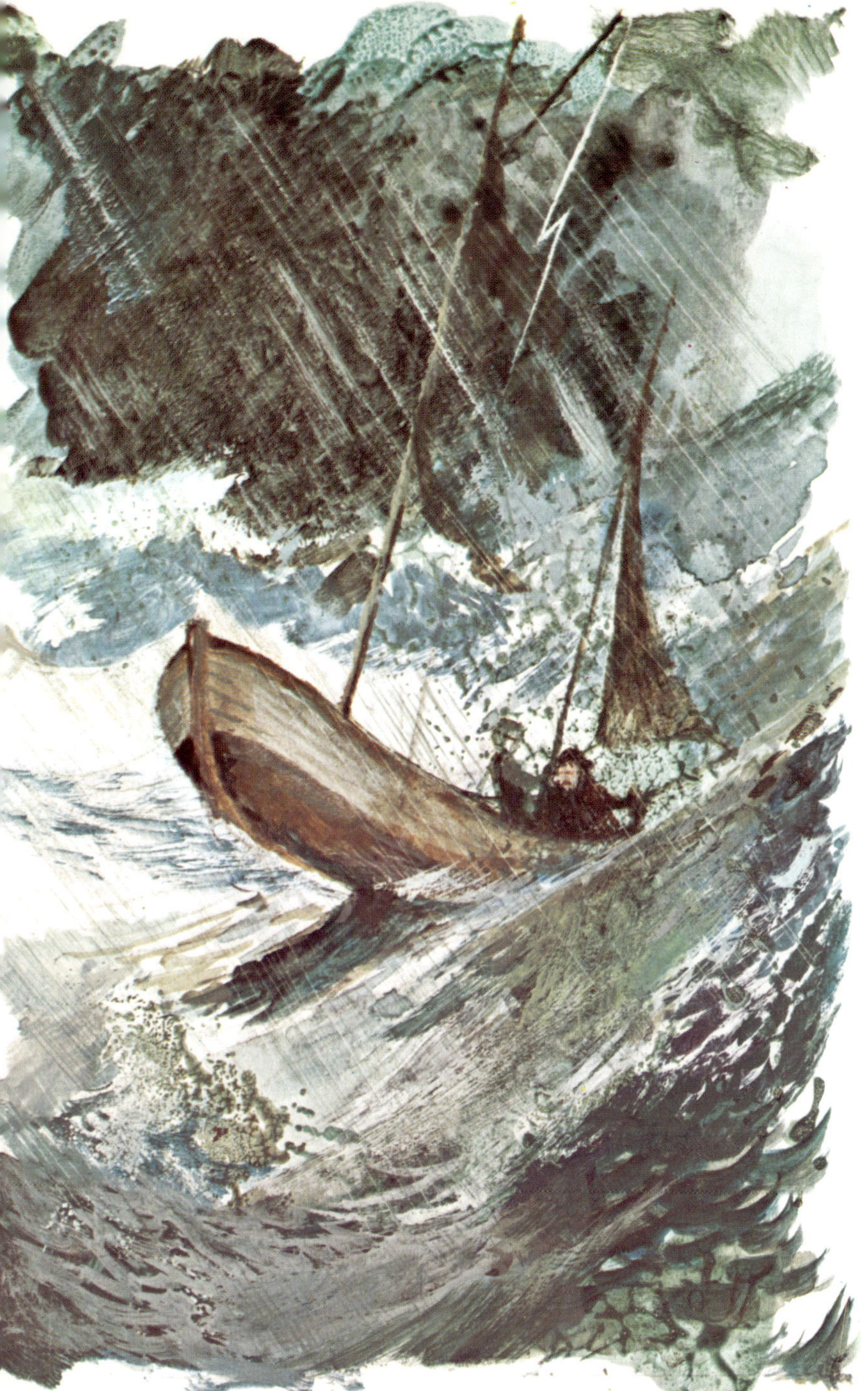

battled with the winds and waves, bailing out the water that poured over the sides, and trying to keep the boat upright. The lantern had fallen long ago and been washed away, but in the flashes of lightning they saw the waves rising like mountains above them. They saw the torn and tattered sails, and each other's wet clothes and pale, anxious faces.

Soon there was an unexpected grinding sound beneath, and the boat came to a sudden stop.

"Land!" gasped the boy in relief, and for a moment he thought they were saved.

"No, not land," murmured the man. "Rocks or a sand bank far out at sea, I'm afraid." He looked at the boy, and knew he was weak with cold and weariness.

"Have courage," he said. "See, the storm is dying down, and daylight will soon be here." He spoke bravely, but in his heart he knew that the poor boat would soon be broken up, and washed away in pieces on the morning tide.

* * * * * *

Morning dawned over Denmark, calm and beautiful. The sun sent a rosy glow over the green fields, and touched the dark forests with the gold of day. The wind and the rain had passed. Only the sea still tossed restlessly, as if remembering the storm of the night before.

Soren Kanne was a farmer. He rose with the dawn, opened the door of his stable, and led his two horses to the field to graze. This was the thing he did first every morning, for the horses were the pride and joy of his life. They were fine creatures, sleek and glossy, with heads held high, and bodies quivering with the excitement of a new day. Soren patted their shiny coats, and stood in the field beside them, gazing out at the sea, and thinking with pity of sailors and fishermen who must have tossed all night in the storm.

But what was that? He shaded his eyes, and looked again. There, leaning over on its side, was a boat stranded on the sandbank. A tattered fragment of sail still clung to the mast, and even from that distance Soren could see waves breaking over the sides in a white fringe of foam.

"Poor fishermen," he thought, "their ship is wrecked, and they are drowned." He gazed sadly across the grey water, and all the joy of the morning was gone. Poor, poor fishermen drowned in the storm and the darkness, with no one near to help them. And now, in a little while, even their boat would be smashed to pieces and hidden for ever in the sea.

Then a new thought came to him. Perhaps the fishermen were *not* drowned. Perhaps one at least was alive, clinging to the wreck, hoping and hoping for help to come. At that moment Soren seemed to see something move on the boat. It may have been a shred of sail blowing, or a piece of wood falling, or a wave breaking. It may have been just his imagination—but it *might* have been a man, alive, and alone out there.

Quickly Soren tried to decide what to do. The man would be too weak to swim, and it would be impossible for Soren to bring him to the land from such a distance. There were no boats near. What could he do? What *could* he do? His horses moved a few steps away, munching at the fresh, dewy grass. They looked so fine, so sleek and glossy. Suddenly Soren knew what to do. The horses could swim. Had they not swum with him when the farm had been flooded? They were strong and powerful. *They* could save the poor fisherman.

Soren called them, and put on their bridles. He

mounted one horse, and holding the rein of the other, he drove them down the sandy beach and into the cold water. The horses were puzzled by this strange command, but they loved and trusted their master, and when they had waded out of their depth, they swam at his bidding. Through the waves they went, swimming farther and farther from the shore, farther and farther out to sea.

Soon Soren could see the ship quite clearly. It was broken and battered, and there amid the wreckage were two people—a boy and a man. They were half asleep now with cold and weariness, and when they saw Soren and the two horses swimming towards them, they thought they must be dreaming. The man came to his senses first, and knew that a rescuer had come at last. He was so glad and grateful that he couldn't speak, couldn't even say thank you to this brave farmer.

"Have you enough strength to cling to my horse?" asked Soren.

The man nodded his head. Soren lifted the boy on to the other horse, helped the man down from the wreck, and gave him a rein to hold. Then the horses started to swim back to the land.

It was a slow journey, for many times Soren had to lean down to prevent the man from slipping, and many times he had to put his arm around the boy to keep him from falling. The horses were strong but their burden was heavy, and they began to grow tired, and to swim more slowly. Soren urged them forward, and at last they reached the shore. They splashed up through the shallow water, and sank down on the sand, with Soren and the boy and the man stretched out exhausted beside them.

Soren looked proudly at the tired horses. How fine they looked lying on the yellow sand, their coats wet and gleaming from the sea. How brave and strong they were —the bravest horses in all Denmark.

And the people of Denmark must have thought so too, for in the little town beside the sea, they put a statue in memory of Soren and his horses, so that even today the story of the shipwreck is told and remembered.

Extract from a Bird Diary

Do you know what a bird diary is? Yes, it is a book in which you keep an account of all the things you see, or find out for yourself about birds. Thus you would enter in your bird diary the names of the different kinds of birds you saw each month—when you heard the first cuckoo, saw the first swallow or spotted the first birds preparing their nests.

It is good fun to keep a bird diary and to make a record of all you can find out about birds. Whether you live in the town or in the country you can find out quite a lot about the bird life in your neighbourhood. If you go away for a holiday, take your bird diary with you, and in your spare time enter some notes on what you have seen, or heard or found in this new district.

In starting a bird diary it is best to get an exercise book with a stiff cover. It is usual, in keeping a diary, to put the date each time you write about something, and it is a good plan also to enter the name of the place at which you have made any very interesting discovery.

You need not carry your diary around with you. All you have to do is to obtain a small note book, which can be carried in your pocket and used whenever you wish to jot something down. Don't forget to put the date each time. Then once a week you can transfer from the small note book to your bird diary all the notes about things of which you really want to keep a record.

You can also make little coloured drawings of some of the birds you see, of their nests and their eggs, of the things they eat and of the places in which they build their nests. It is most interesting to be able to read your diary from the previous winter, or spring or summer, and to compare what you wrote then with what is happening now.

Here is part of a bird diary kept by Malcolm, who was eleven years old when he wrote these notes.

This part of his diary was headed:
"White Tip the Missel Thrush"

April 4th
While I was playing in Dingle Wood, I was just about to climb a tree when I turned round and saw, facing me, a missel thrush who sat on her nest as still as stone.

The nest, which was open, was situated just over a metre from the ground, and it was lined with grass and hay.

My friend and I decided to leave White Tip, as we agreed to call her, to sit on her nest.

We called her White Tip because she had a white tip at the end of her tail.

April 4th (afternoon)
This afternoon I was going to call for my friend when

I saw White Tip sitting in a meadow preening her feathers.

So I went to her nest and found three blind balls of fluff and, to my amazement, an infertile egg. I could tell it was infertile because it was transparent. The egg was bluish-brown with delicate clove-brown markings.

April 5th
This afternoon I took my mother and father and sister to see White Tip's nest. At first they couldn't see her because she stuck her head up in the air as if to resemble the surrounding twigs. When my father tried to stroke her, she nipped his fingers. In the end she flew off to a nearby tree from which she started scolding us. My sister was very excited and wanted to take a baby home, but I wouldn't let her. After viewing White Tip's babies we went home.

April 6th
Today I went to White Tip's nest to try to draw her babies. They were still blind. I saw White Tip and her mate, Hop, as I decided to call him.

April 8th
Today I watched White Tip's babies being fed. White Tip let her babies pull a worm out of her beak. When they opened their mouths, they showed wide throats. They were very hungry!

April 9th
Today I went to see White Tip's babies and they seem to be increasing in size. They are losing their fluffiness and are growing feathers.

April 10th
When I went to see the babies, White Tip dived down at me from the branch of a tree. She kept on swooping at me until I went away from her nest.

Her babies are still blind and their feathers are growing bigger.

The babies are so big that they are nearly falling out of the nest. White Tip can hardly sit on them, they are so big.

April 11th
Today, the eighth day, White Tip's babies opened their eyes. White Tip again swooped down at me. The babies' feathers have grown still more.

April 15th
White Tip's babies are nearly ready to fly as their feathers are nearly full grown.

She kept swooping down at me when I went near the nest. I thought when I approached the tree that White Tip was on the nest, but I was surprised to find that it was one of her youngsters.

April 16th
I am afraid that today is the last time I shall see White Tip's nest as I have to return home. When I went near the fence to see the nest, White Tip attacked me. I could not see it but I think her youngsters will fly in a few days.

April 23rd
Today I received a letter from my friend saying that White Tip had reared her young successfully and that they had all flown away.

The Boy who Set the Birds Free

The sun danced in and out among the grape vines of Italy, making little patterns of light and shade upon the path where Leonardo walked long ago. Two butterflies chased each other above the clusters of green grapes, and a small, brown lizard darted swiftly out from under a stone.

Leonardo noticed everything—the grapes, the sunshine, the butterflies and the lizard, but he went on thinking about a new kind of paint he had been mixing that morning. It was blue, deep and clear. It would be beautiful for pictures of flowers and angels' eyes, or for skies and tossing seas.

The path led to a stream. Leonardo stopped on the bank a moment to watch a beetle open its gauzy wings. Then he sat down on the grass, and gazed into the water, fascinated by the swirl of tiny whirlpools around water-lily leaves, and the curve of the ripples as they tumbled over the stones.

"Leonardo!" called a voice. "Leonardo!"

His friend Paolo came running through the vineyard, and sat down beside him.

"You know," said Leonardo thoughtfully, without looking up, "it ought to be possible to make a boat to travel under water."

"It wouldn't work," laughed Paolo. "The sails would get wet." (Those were the days of sailing boats.)

"Sails!" repeated Leonardo scornfully. "It wouldn't have sails. It would have some sort of machine inside it. I don't quite know how it would work, but I know it would be possible. I must draw a plan of an underwater boat when I get home."

"You think of such strange things," said Paolo. "Come to the market with me. I have to return this lute to a man there. My father has been mending it for him."

Leonardo looked up with interest.

"A lute!" he exclaimed. "Let me try it."

He took the lute from Paolo, plucked at the strings with his thumb and finger, and then played a gay tune.

"I didn't know you could play," said Paolo in surprise. "How long have you been learning?"

"I haven't learnt at all. I've never even tried a lute before."

"But you can play it as well as my father."

Leonardo played again. His eyes became dreamy. His thoughts wandered far away, and from Paolo's lute he drew most wonderful music. Paolo sat amazed, staring at Leonardo, and listening to the soft sweetness of the tune as it went sighing over the stream, and whispering through the vines.

How clever Leonardo was, he thought. Most children were clever at one or two things, but Leonardo seemed to be clever at everything he tried. He was handsome to look upon, and he could draw and paint as well as some of the most famous artists in Italy. He knew the names of all the flowers and all the birds; all the insects that hid in the grass, and all the stars that shone in the sky. He could make up poetry, and carve people from lumps of stone. He could work out the most difficult sums, and he understood all about medicine, and the bones and muscles of the human body. He invented clever machines, and toys that worked. He could win any running race, and jump higher than any other boy. He was so strong that he could straighten an iron horseshoe with his hands. Yet he was so gentle that he would not hurt any living thing. Even flowers could feel pain, he said, and he would step aside so that his foot should not crush them.

Sometimes Paolo and Leonardo and their friends talked about what they would be when they grew older. One said he would be a builder, and another a farmer, but Leonardo said something different every time— an artist, a doctor, an engineer, an architect, a musician, a poet. Leonardo could choose from everything in the world.

"Come," said Paolo, interrupting the music at last. "I must go."

So Leonardo returned the lute, and walked beside his friend to the village and the market-place.

There were animals in the market, waiting to be sold. Shabby, grey donkeys were fastened to fences, and weary cows stood mooing mournfully. Leonardo looked at them with pity. Their eyes were so sad, and so full of fear. He spoke gentle words of comfort to them, and wished and wished that he could do something to help them.

Meanwhile Paolo hurried over to a fruit stall, where he could see the man he was seeking. He gave him the lute, and the man smiled, and plucked eagerly at the strings.

"Ah! I am glad to have it back again," he said. "Please thank your father very much for mending it."

"Yes," answered Paolo, and looking round for his

friend, he added,

"Leonardo can play the lute."

"Leonardo is a wonderful boy," was the reply. "Such children are born only once in a thousand years."

By this time Leonardo was wandering among the stalls, looking here and there, interested in everything. Then he saw something that filled him with horror. He saw birds in cages—wild birds in small, wooden cages, where they had scarcely room to stretch their wings.

"Oh!" whispered Leonardo, and though the sun beat down upon him, he turned icy cold. Birds were meant to fly. The whole wide sky was made for their fluttering wings. And here were birds being sold in cages—each one a prisoner and alone. With sorrowing eyes Leonardo gazed at them. Some were beating themselves against the bars, trying desperately to escape. Some chirped and chirped, still expecting every moment to be set free. Some huddled down as far away as possible, silent and hopeless. Leonardo saw the beating of their hearts, and the shivering of their feathers. He saw the hope and the despair in their eyes. His heart was filled with pity.

On the way home he was unusually quiet.

"What are you planning now?" asked Paolo.

"Nothing."

"Is anything wrong then?"

"There were birds in cages at the market," burst out Leonardo angrily. "Birds in prison when they should be free. Oh, Paolo, how cruel and wicked some people are!"

Leonardo was unhappy nearly all day. There were lots of things he meant to do. He wanted to draw a picture of water rushing in a torrent of ripples and curves, bubbling over rocks, and swirling round reeds. Then he wanted to paint it with his new blue paint. He meant to make a plan for a boat that would travel under the sea. He intended to ask Paolo's father for a piece of wood to make a lute for himself.

But when he started the water picture, he found himself drawing a bird, and when he began the plan of the under-water boat, he found himself sketching wings. And when he went out of doors, to walk to Paolo's house, he seemed to see again those sad, imprisoned birds.

At that moment a man from a neighbouring house came along the road, carrying a shield. He stopped and spoke to Leonardo.

"That's a nice shield," remarked the boy.

"Yes. It's a new one."

"It only needs a picture painted on it now."

"Yes. A picture of a dragon would look fine, wouldn't it?"

"If you like," offered Leonardo, "I'll paint one for you."

"Will you?" cried the man in delight. Eagerly he handed over the shield, adding,

"I'll pay you for your work."

Leonardo went into the house again, and sat down to practise drawing a dragon on paper, so that he would be able to do it really well on the shield. He wished he had a real dragon to copy, but dragons of course were only fairy tale creatures, and no one had ever seen one. He made several attempts, but none of them satisfied him. He liked to understand how things were made before he tried to draw them. For instance, before he drew a leaf, he studied every little vein in it, and before he drew a cat, he felt its body gently so that he knew the position of all its bones. It was a pity he couldn't study a dragon.

Suddenly an idea came to him. He ran to the vineyard, and explored the banks of the stream. He wandered round the hillside, and peeped into a cave among the boulders. When he returned to the house again, he took with him a strange assortment of creatures. There were a lizard, a butterfly, a grasshopper, a bat and a cricket. He carried them so carefully that they seemed to know he wouldn't harm them.

"Now" said Leonardo, arranging them on the floor. "The leathery wing of a bat must be something like the wing of a dragon, and the thick, cold skin of this little lizard must be something like a dragon's skin." So he copied part of one creature, and part of another, getting a little help from each in turn, until he was quite sure he could make a real dragon.

By the time the dragon on the shield was finished, and Leonardo had taken the little wild creatures back to their homes, evening had come, and it was getting dark. Leonardo propped the shield up against the wall of the room. It certainly was a fine dragon. Its leathery wings were half open. It breathed fire from its mouth, and it looked very fierce!

Soon Leonardo's father came home. As he entered the darkening room, he came face to face with a pair of flashing eyes, and he stepped back almost in alarm.

"Oh, Father!" laughed Leonardo. "I believe my dragon frightened you just for a second."

"He's enough to give anyone a shock," was the reply. "What a fierce dragon he is! You've painted him well, Leonardo. He looks as if he's alive. You'd better be an artist when you grow up."

Leonardo smiled. "I think I'd rather be a chemist, or study the stars," he said. "And I've just had an idea for making a machine to lift heavy weights. Tomorrow I'll write a description of it."

It was only when Leonardo was in bed that night that he remembered again the unhappy birds beating their wings against bars in the market.

In the morning the dragon was dry. His eyes shone fiercely. His paint gleamed in the sunshine. He looked ready to pounce right off the shield if anyone were to come near.

Directly after breakfast Leonardo took the shield to its owner. The man was delighted with the dragon, and he dropped some money into Leonardo's hand.

Leonardo was very pleased. He called for his friend Paolo, saying,

"Come with me to the market. I have money to spend."

"What will you buy?" asked Paolo, as they walked along the road to the village. "They had good cakes there yesterday—or are you going to buy fruit?"

"I haven't decided yet," said Leonardo, but though he did decide suddenly a moment later, he did not tell his plan to Paolo. When they reached the market, however, he went straight to the stall where the caged birds had been. Yes, there were still some there—sad little wild birds that should have been singing in the tree tops on this beautiful summer day.

"How many birds can I buy with this?" asked Leonardo, holding out his money.

"I'll let you have two," replied the stall holder.

Leonardo paid the money, and walked away carrying two cages—with two little birds fluttering in renewed fear at the sudden movement. Paolo was puzzled.

"You say it's wicked to sell wild birds in the market," he said, "and yet you buy them yourself."

Leonardo smiled, and gave no answer. But he spoke gently to the imprisoned birds, and they ceased their anxious flutterings as if they trusted him.

A little later the boys climbed a winding, hillside path, and sat down to rest. The market place with its sounds and voices seemed far away. Up here there was nothing to disturb the beauty of the morning. A quiet breeze swayed the grasses, and busy insects hummed in and out of nodding flowers. Above, the sky was cloudless, and as blue as Leonardo had ever known it.

"Just the right sort of day," he remarked as he set the two wooden cages down on the grass, and opened wide the doors.

"Oh," murmured Paolo, "I ought to have guessed," and he kept very still, watching.

At first the birds did not understand that they could walk out of their cages. They seemed afraid to try. Then, as courage and hope grew, they hopped to the doors, and then slowly out on to the ground. They felt grass beneath their feet. They saw space and sky above. They fluttered their feathers and opened their wings, and closed them again. Then they spread them wide, and rose into the air—up and up and up in the blue sky.

Leonardo and Paolo watched, holding back their heads, and following the flight with their eyes. The birds circled twice above the village, hovering for a moment over a group of tall trees. Then they flew away and away till they became as specks in the distance, and then they were lost to sight in the blue of the sky.

"Now they're happy," whispered Leonardo joyfully. "Oh, whenever I have money I'll buy little birds in cages, and set them free."

That afternoon, sitting by the stream with Paolo, he drew birds' wings. He knew just how the bones and muscles worked, and he understood exactly how a bird turned, or flew higher or lower. Paolo watched in admiration. How wonderful were the drawings of Leonardo da Vinci!

"You know," said Leonardo suddenly, "if birds can fly, why shouldn't people?"

"People have no wings," answered Paolo.

"They could build wings. I've a fine idea for making a flying machine. Look!" He started to draw again with swift, eager strokes—and there among the vineyards of Italy, he made what was perhaps the first plan of a flying machine in the world. Then he lay back on the grass and closed his eyes, and the stream bubbled on over the stones, and the air was filled with the singing of birds—wild birds, happy and free.

The story of Leonardo da Vinci is very long, too long

to be told in a short story like this.

While he was still a boy, he went as a pupil to a famous artist named Verrochio. Very soon Verrochio discovered that his pupil needed little teaching, and could paint much better than he himself.

So time passed and Leonardo grew up to become the wonder of his age. Year by year he worked and worked, living day and night in his studio. He seldom slept or relaxed. There was always something to be done. And even before one task was finished, his brilliant, restless brain would be urging him on to try out another idea. He filled notebooks with drawings of animals and flowers and people, and plans of buildings, machinery and inventions. He wrote about winds and clouds, painting and poetry. He was a musician, an astronomer, chemist, mathematician. He could do all things well. Leonardo had more natural gifts than any man before or since.

But in a life of ever changing interest, there were two things which he seemed to like to study, write about, and draw most of all—water and wings.

Perhaps he remembered the little stream near the vineyard, where he watched the swirl of tiny whirlpools round water-lily leaves, and the curve of the ripples as they tumbled over the stones. Perhaps he remembered the first time he bought birds in cages from the market (and oh, how many times he had done it since!).

Perhaps he remembered the beating of their wings as they flew away when he set them free—away and away till they became as specks in the distance, and then were lost to sight in the blue of the sky.

Leonardo da Vinci

He was born in 1452.

He died in 1519. How old was he?

Two of his best known pictures are:

Mona Lisa—a portrait of a woman with a strange smile.
The Last Supper—a Bible picture.

Here are two of Leonardo's riddles. Can you guess the answers?

1. What is it that is much desired by men, but which they know not while possessing?
2. Which men will take pleasure in seeing their own works worn out and destroyed?

You will find the answers on page 78.

The Magic Doors

There are buildings in some towns with doors that slide open by themselves when anyone approaches them. People sometimes look round in surprise, wondering how the doors open and how they know just when to do it. It seems like magic!

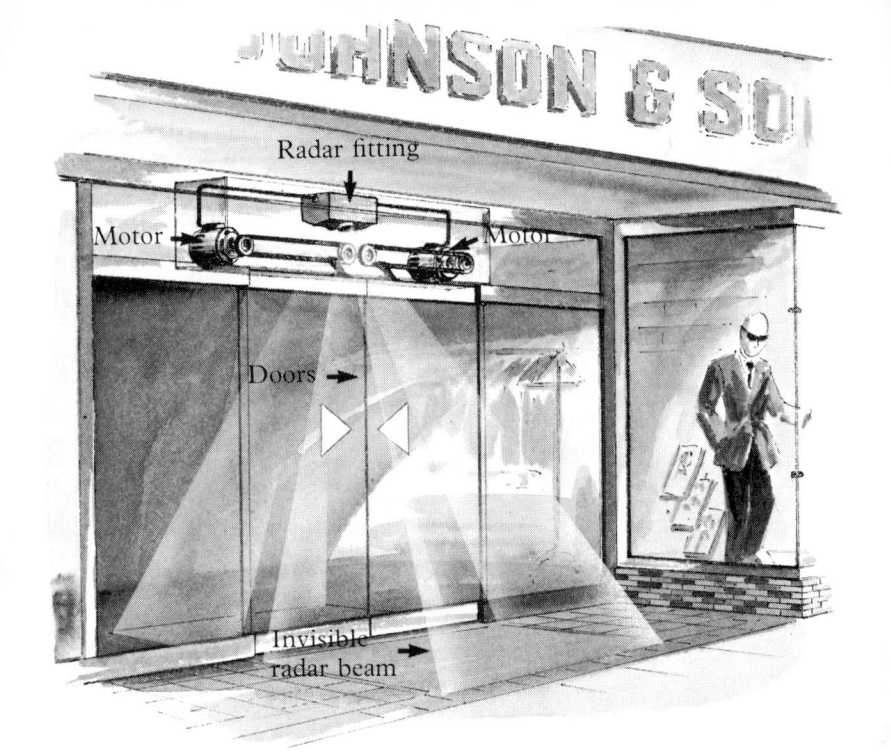

The magic is really a clever use of an invisible beam known as a radar beam. This beam is sent out from a fitting which looks rather like a wall light and which is fixed over the doors. Whenever people approach the doors they step into the invisible beam. The beam is disturbed and this causes an electric motor to be switched on. This motor pulls the doors open and holds them open for as long as the beam is disturbed.

When the person steps out of the beam the motor switches off and the doors are allowed to close.

It may not be real magic, but it's almost as good, isn't it?

The Champion

It was because of his bicycle that Cassius Clay learned how to fight. Or rather it was because his bicycle was stolen!

Cassius was twelve years old at the time. He lived in the town of Louisville in the USA, where he was born to poor, black parents in 1942.

He was very much like any other boy of his age. He went to school, because he had to, but he preferred playing games with his friends. Cassius was always popular because he was good at sports. He was a useful person to have in your team—he liked to win! With his friends he spent a good deal of time at the local sports centre in Louisville, and it was from there that his bicycle was stolen.

His bicycle was the most important thing that Cassius owned. It had cost his parents money which they could not easily afford, and now someone had taken it. Cassius was angry. He was very angry indeed, and very unhappy.

When he found that the bicycle had gone he stormed back into the sports centre in a furious mood. But none of his friends had seen the bicycle or knew who had taken it.

"I'll murder him," shouted Cassius. "I'll murder him when I find him!"

"Don't do that!" laughed the man who ran the boys' club at the centre. "I'd only have to arrest you." He worked as a policeman during the day.

"But what about my bike?" shouted Cassius. "Can't you help me get it back?"

The policeman shook his head. "It's difficult to find a stolen bike," he said. "And the police have more important things to do. You'll have to look for it yourself. But if you do find it, I'll show you how to teach the thief a lesson he won't forget in a hurry!" He took Cassius into the gym and helped him to put on a pair of boxing gloves, and there and then he gave him his first lesson in how to fight.

Cassius learned quickly. It was not long before he began to realise that boxing was the sport he enjoyed most. The policeman taught him all he knew, and arranged for him to fight other boys. As Cassius grew bigger and stronger he won more and more fights. The only thing he wanted to do when he left school was to be a boxer. It was the one sport at which very few people could beat him.

His father and mother were not at all happy about this. Cassius was a clever boy and they wanted him to train for a good job. His father had hoped that he would go to college and become a teacher, but Cassius wanted none of it. By the time he was sixteen his greatest ambition was to join the American team that would box in the Olympic Games in Rome two years later. He was determined to win the highest award they could give him, the Olympic Gold Medal.

"I'm going to bring home that medal," said Cassius. "I am going to show everyone that I am the greatest there is." His family knew that when Cassius made up his mind to do something, he meant it!

For two years he trained long and hard. In the end his ambition was realised. He *was* chosen for the team that went to Rome and he *did* come home with the precious medal. Cassius left America as a young man whom nobody knew. By the time he went back home to Louisville from the Rome Olympics, he was a hero.

From then on everyone wanted to watch him fight. More and more matches were arranged for him, and large sums of money were paid out. Cassius worked hard and developed his strength and skill. At the same time he developed a style and a way of talking that soon earned him the nickname of the Louisville Lip!

"I'm going to be the greatest there is," he had boasted at sixteen.

"I *AM* the greatest!" he told them three years later. He boasted about his skills and annoyed people so much that they paid more and more money just to see if someone could beat him. But Cassius was never beaten. He skipped round and round the ring, as light on his feet as a dancer, teasing the men he fought.

"Float like a butterfly, sting like a bee," he said, and that was how it must have seemed to the men who climbed into the ring to fight him. Cassius went on to bigger and better fights. At last in 1964 he beat the American boxer Sonny Liston and became World Champion.

"Now tell me," he shouted at the pressmen afterwards, "who is the greatest?"

"You are!" they shouted back.

But his biggest fight was still to come. Three days after he became World Champion he announced that he had joined a religious group called the Black Muslims, and had changed his name to Muhammad Ali. Because of his religion he refused to join the American army who were fighting in Vietnam, even when ordered to by the Government. So they took away from him the title of World Champion and refused to let him box in America. For three years Ali fought a legal battle in the courts. In the end, as determined as ever, he won the right to be a boxer again.

But it took a long time for Muhammad Ali to win back his title. He lost the first time he tried, fighting against Joe Frazier. People said that he had been away from boxing for three years and was really too old. But he never gave up. He went on training and after three more years, in 1974, he came face to face with George Foreman, who had won the title from Frazier.

They met in the African country of Zaire. Thousands of people came to watch the fight. Round the world, millions more sat by their television sets, watching.

The two American boxers fought grimly. It was a hard fight and they were evenly matched. The huge crowd, shouting and yelling, urged on the man who had once been champion. Ali shook his head clear and fought on, but he seemed to be slower and more tired. Then suddenly, as the bell rang for the start of Round Eight, he came out of his corner dancing on his toes. The old Ali was back, determined to finish it there and then. One massive swing with his right arm and the fight was over.

George Foreman fell to his back on the canvas floor of the ring—and stayed there.

The crowd went wild. They screamed their joy, threw their arms around each other and surged forward to see the winner. Ali stood in the ring, under the brilliant lights and stared out over the sea of faces. Again and again they shouted "Ali! Champion! Ali! Champion!" Their shouts rang out from television sets and radios all round the world. Muhammad Ali, the boy who had learned to fight in the gym of the Louisville sports centre was back on top again. His name flashed round the world on every morning paper.

Ali had won back his World Champion crown.

Moira Miller

Answers to page 69.   1. Sleep.   2. Shoemakers.

The Run for Oklahoma

The children sat in the doorway and watched their father ride across the prairie. He turned once and waved to them. Then he galloped faster and faster into the distance.

"Jancy's a racehorse all right," remarked Elmer.

"Yes," said Chris, "but I guess he never had to run a race that meant so much to anyone as the Oklahoma race will mean to us."

Curly and Kit, two sturdy little boys of five and four, went inside the almost empty shack, and stamped up and down on the wooden floors, laughing with delight at the noisy echoes.

"Oh, we *must* win," murmured Chris, shading her eyes from the sun as she watched Father taking Jancy for a final practice run.

The Oklahoma land had belonged to the American Indians, but the Government had bought part of it, and was throwing it open to white settlers. It had been marked off into sections, each one eighty hectares in size. Anyone could claim a section, free of charge, on April the twenty-second at twelve o'clock midday. Already families were travelling towards the starting line, planning to make farms, planning to build homes—if only they could run fast enough to stake their claims at the appointed time!

"How I wish tomorrow were here," sighed Elmer, who was twelve. "Then at least we'd be on our way."

"Father's out of sight now," murmured Chris. (She was eleven.) "He went at a fine speed. There can't be many better horsemen than Father anyway, nor many better horses than Jancy."

Father had sold up nearly everything so that he might buy Jancy. He had kept only an arm chair for Mother, three mattresses for the children to share, a few pots and pans and blankets—and of course the cart and Dapple, the slow old horse who pulled it. With the money he had bought a large tent and Jancy, who had once been a racehorse.

"When we've staked our claim and built our farmhouse," he had said, "we'll sell Jancy, and buy back our furniture. I guess we'll do fine in Oklahoma."

It was unfortunate that Mother had become ill with fever at that time, and been taken away to be nursed. So all the clearing of the shack as well as the cooking, and the caring for Curly and Kit, had fallen upon Elmer and Chris.

"I guess we'd better do something about dinner," said Elmer, "or Father will be back before it's ready."

"Our last dinner here," said Chris with a hop of excitement. "Tomorrow we'll be on the way."

Soon the food was cooked and dinner was prepared, but Father hadn't returned.

"He's a long while," remarked Chris. She looked at her two small brothers, and sighed. As soon as she washed them, they seemed to get dirty again. "Oh, Curly, do wash your hands—and you, Kit."

"Let's start," said Elmer. "We'll heat Father's dinner again when he comes."

The meal was finished, and the afternoon passed slowly away. Elmer cut chips off a stick with his knife. Chris lay dreaming in the shadow of a tree. Curly and Kit, tired out from romping and laughing together, had stretched out on a mattress and fallen asleep.

A stranger on a black horse rode across the prairie, with a second horse on a leading rein. Elmer looked up, and his sunburnt cheeks turned suddenly pale. Chris sat up slowly, and fear clutched at her heart. The horse on the leading rein was Jancy. Where was Father?

"Is your name Graham?" shouted the stranger.

"Yes," answered Elmer in a queer, tight voice that didn't sound like his own.

"This is your father's horse then, isn't it?"

The two children were up on their feet now. The man dismounted, and pushed back his broad-brimmed hat.

"I've bad news for you," he said.

Chris opened her mouth to speak, but no words came. The stranger put a kindly arm round her shoulder.

"Your father had a fall," he continued. "I'm afraid his leg is broken, and he's badly shaken. It happened up near my farm. My partner has taken him to hospital. He'll have to be there some weeks I guess. But don't you worry. He'll be all right."

Elmer said nothing. His heart was beating like a hammer against his chest. Chris stared at the stranger, and was certain she was dreaming. She felt so queer and far away.

"He'll be all right," said the stranger again. "And I guess you'll manage to look after yourselves till he's better, won't you? By the way, he sent a special message for you—said I was to be sure not to forget it. I wrote it down." He fumbled in his pocket, and brought out a crumpled bit of paper. "Yes, here it is—'Tell Elmer and Chris,' he said, 'that it all depends on them now.'"

Inside the shack Curly awoke and slid along the mattress till his feet touched the floor. Then he started drumming with his heels in faint, regular beats.

"Oh, well, I must get back," said the stranger, giving Jancy's rein to Elmer, and mounting the black horse. "You'll be all right, won't you? Remember what your father said.—It all depends on you now."

He touched his hat, waved his hand, and galloped back across the prairie.

"You know what Father meant," said Elmer, finding his voice at last. Chris gulped.

"Oklahoma," she whispered.

★ ★ ★ ★ ★ ★

So that was how it was that the Graham family started the journey to the Oklahoma lands next day, with no mother to look after them, and no father to stake their claim.

Chris drove the cart, pulled at a slow but steady trot by Dapple. In the cart were the three mattresses and Mother's arm chair, tied over the top with a great curve of string. In the cart too were the blankets, the tent, the pots and pans, and a store of food and water; and jogging up and down among these poor possessions were Curly and Kit, already untidy and covered in dust.

At the side rode Elmer on Jancy.

"No chance of missing the way now," said Elmer after a few hours. "Look."

There ahead was a long line of horsemen, of shabby carts, covered wagons and every queer construction that could be dragged on two wheels or more. There were other families from all the states of North America, following the dusty trail to seek homes in Oklahoma.

There was plenty of company on the roadside that night as the children stopped to rest; and even when the sun went down, the air was as hot as it had been by day. Anxious to make an early start next morning, the children decided not to pitch the tent. Instead, they curled up together on the pile of mattresses in the cart; and Elmer, Chris, Curly and Kit slept beneath the moon.

Next day they went on again, driving steadily, and stopping only for food, or to let Curly and Kit stretch their cramped legs. Many horses and wagons overtook them, for Dapple was slow. Curly amused himself by counting all the people who waved to the little family, or who shouted encouragement as they passed.

In the afternoon the journey's end was reached. There were the homeseekers, camped at the edge of the Oklahoma lands. There were hundreds of carts, wagons, tents and horses, and thousands of men, women and children.

"Oh, *look* at them all!" said Chris, disappointment creeping into her voice. She had hoped that there would not be very many after all—that by some stroke of luck there might be only as many people as there were sections to claim.

"Wherever shall we camp?" she added. Elmer looked round slowly before he answered.

"Over there by those trees. I can see a space just about big enough."

Soon Chris was holding the tent pole, and Elmer was hammering tent pegs into the hard earth. Curly and Kit wandered to a covered wagon, and stared quite openly at a woman who sat beside it. She was doing needlework, as if she were comfortably seated in an ordinary garden. Two men came over to help with the tent, and then to admire Jancy.

Elmer and Chris sat down at last to refresh themselves with water, bread and jam. Curly and Kit ran up at once, and flopped down on the grass beside them.

"What a lot of tents and wagons," said Curly, pushing his loose, untidy curls out of his eyes.

"I'm hungry," said Kit, cramming bread and jam into his mouth with more speed than manners. The two little boys were quite happy, thinking only of the fun of the moment. But Elmer and Chris gazed across at the Oklahoma lands, and thought with hope and fear of the race to be run. The land was rather bare, except where a few trees and bushes clustered round a trickling stream in the distance. A soldier on horseback rode by, keeping over-anxious people away from the edge; and far away a prairie wolf slunk into a patch of long grass.

April the twenty-second was still two days ahead—two long days. Curly and Kit made friends with other children, and romped and played, and became more tousled and dirty than ever. Elmer and Chris prepared simple meals, and did all the odd jobs about their camp. They listened to groups of men talking, and became friendly with some people who had camped near by. A motherly woman with a crate of clucking hens gave two new-laid eggs to Chris. A tall, serious man gave Elmer a sharpened stake with which to stake his claim. Elmer carved "Graham" on it with his knife.

"We're lucky to have Jancy," he said to Chris. "Some people are paying to hire racehorses just for the day."

"Someone said there are more than twenty thousand people here," said Chris. "That means that lots of them will be unlucky. The man in the next wagon says that if he doesn't get a claim, he'll stay around for a week or two in case anyone wants to sell their claim to him."

"I wonder which is the best way to run," murmured Elmer. "I've asked lots of people. One man said ride north, but another said ride to trees, because if there are trees, there must be water. I've been thinking, Chris—if I stake my claim, and then come back for you and the others, someone *might* steal my claim."

"Yes," put in Chris with an anxious nod of her head. "You stake the claim and find the corner stones, and I'll follow with the children and the cart, and the tent and everything. Most of the women are following up their husbands."

April the twenty-second came at last. Long before dawn the children had taken down the tent, and packed it with the mattresses and Mother's arm chair and all the other things in the cart. Elmer had stuffed his pockets with food, and hung a water bottle on his belt. With his stake in his hand he had taken his place on the starting line with Jancy. Soldiers rode backwards and forwards, keeping the course clear. At twelve o'clock they would fire their guns and the race would start. But it was a long time yet till twelve o'clock.

There were all sorts of people on the starting line, thousands of them—people on horses, people in covered wagons, people in carts, professional runners on their own feet.

"You're hopeful, aren't you?" said a great bronzed horseman to a thin little man in running shoes.

"Ah! Don't you worry," he replied with a grin. "While your horse is prancing all over the prairie, I shall slip away to the side, and stake one of the claims you pass."

"Yes, but they say the richest land is farther over."

"This is rich enough for me. I'm going to build a store."

So the morning passed, slowly, slowly. The sun beat down in fierce splendour. People who owned watches brought them out every few minutes. Elmer, in his nervousness and excitement, asked the time more often than he realised.

"Oh, don't keep asking the time," said someone. "You make it go more slowly."

At last the soldiers rode forward and stood some distance away, waiting for twelve o'clock.

"How old are you, son?" asked a man in a covered wagon.

"Twelve," said Elmer.

"And who are you running for?"

"My mother and father. They're both in hospital."

"Well, I hope you get a good claim. Good luck to you, kid."

In the line of families at the back, Chris sat in the cart, holding Dapple's rein.

"Dapple," she said, "you're not going in for the race, but all the same you must run faster than you've ever run before, so that I can keep Elmer in sight."

Curly and Kit ran round and round the wagon, shrieking with excitement.

"I think you'd better come up now," said Chris, leaning over to help them. "When we start, you'll sit still, won't you? Hold on tightly, and watch Elmer all the time."

A silence had crept along the starting line. Elmer sat high on Jancy now, and didn't dare to ask the time. He wore a scarlet shirt and a large, cowboy hat that belonged to Father.

"Five to twelve," said someone in a croaky whisper. "Five to twelve."

"Tell Elmer and Chris"—Father had said—"that it all depends on them now."

In the far distance, on a piece of rising ground, a prairie wolf appeared, and stood for a moment like a statue. Then it disappeared.

"It all depends on me," thought Elmer to himself. "It all depends on me."

"Three minutes," murmured a man in a covered wagon.

"Two minutes by my watch," hissed the stout-hearted runner.

"It all depends on me," thought Elmer. "It all depends on me."

A sudden crack of gunfire! Twelve o'clock! Though the crowds had waited for it, the sound startled them. Jancy reared his head, and Elmer gave a little murmur of surprise. The line broke in a cloud of dust. Everyone surged forward—horses, covered wagons, carts, runners. As far as the eye could see—to the right, to the left—horses were galloping, galloping, galloping, urged on feverishly by desperate riders—riding for homes in the Oklahoma lands.

Behind them came the wagons and the families, wheels creaking, children shouting, dogs barking.

With her lips pressed together in determination, and her eyes on the surging line ahead, Chris drove Dapple and the shabby cart. She could see Elmer in his scarlet shirt and his cowboy hat. He was keeping up well. The line was irregular now, like a great curving wave. Some riders were outpacing the others. Some were being left behind. But Elmer in his scarlet shirt and cowboy hat—Elmer was keeping ahead.

"Elmer's winning!" cried Curly, jogging up and down on a mattress.

"Elmer's winning!" echoed Kit.

"Gee up, Dapple, gee up," said Chris.

There was Elmer, only a gleam of scarlet now, in a cloud of dust. He was riding well. But at that very moment Jancy's foot caught in a hole, and he stumbled. Off came Elmer, rolling over and over on the ground.

"Oh!" cried Chris in terror—for like a charging army came the horses behind—surging past and over Elmer. Surely he would be crushed to death by horses' hooves and wagon wheels!

"He's fallen!" wailed Curly.

"He's dead!" screamed Kit.

But Elmer, bruised a little, and covered in dust, was up on his feet again, and mounting Jancy. Once more he urged him forward. Once more he plunged on—faster, faster! He had lost ground, but he was catching up again, passing the swaying wagons and the creaking carts, passing the slower horsemen—catching up, catching up again.

"He's winning again," cried Curly in delight, jogging up and down so much that Mother's armchair began to sway with the movement.

"I can see Elmer," shrieked Kit. "He's winning! He's winning!"

Chris blinked her eyes in the burning sun, and stared at that scarlet shirt in the distance. Elmer might not be winning, but he was keeping ahead, and he ought to get a claim.

Now the distance between the racers and the families became greater. Many of the horsemen rode over the horizon and out of sight. Many of the wagons couldn't keep up the pace. The homeseekers were scattered far and wide all over the prairie, pressing on and pressing forward, each at his own speed. And the prairie wolves ran in terror through the long grass, and the bright prairie flowers were covered in the dust that hung like a cloud above the land.

Elmer was gone now. Somewhere in the distance he was still urging Jancy forward. There was not a glimpse of his scarlet shirt and his cowboy hat.

Dapple was getting tired, being quite unused to running at such a speed, and the most Chris could get from her now was a slow, steady trot.

One by one the wagons and carts dropped out of the run, as their drivers sighted husbands and brothers staking their claims. One by one the families stopped on the eighty hectares of land that were now their own. Mothers and children jumped down to earth, and helped to search for the corner stones in the long grass.

But Chris and Curly and Kit rode on, looking for Elmer. Perhaps he hadn't managed to stake a claim after all. Or perhaps he had, and he was waiting somewhere. Chris began to wonder if she would ever find him. She had seen him ride straight into the distance. The prairie was so vast. He might have gone north or east or west. He might be anywhere.

She came to a family digging a well.

"Please, have you seen a boy on a horse? He was wearing a scarlet shirt and a cowboy hat."

"No. I'm afraid we've been too busy to notice," said one of them.

On trotted Dapple, pulling the creaking cart over the rough ground.

"Where's Elmer?" demanded Curly.

"I'm tired," said Kit.

They came to a man digging a ditch round the edge of his claim.

"Please, have you seen a boy on a horse? He was wearing a scarlet shirt and a cowboy hat."

The man stopped digging, and shook his head.

"Sorry," he said. "I haven't."

On drove Chris for hours and hours. She asked everyone she passed, but they had all seen so many horses—how could they remember, or even notice Elmer?

Tents were set up in the sun. Women made tea over camp fires. Family parties gathered round to refresh themselves. Some men even marked out the foundations for the homes they would build—or began to erect wooden shacks they had brought out in sections.

"I want Elmer," wailed Curly.

"I'm hungry," murmured Kit.

Chris felt desperate. Perhaps she wouldn't find Elmer at all. Perhaps he had fallen, and been killed. Perhaps he hadn't been able to make a claim, and had gone back to camp again behind the starting line. Perhaps she would never find him. She wanted to cry, for she was worn out with the weariness and excitement and hard work of the past few weeks. But if she cried, Curly would cry, and if Curly cried, Kit would cry—and what would be the good of that?

She came to a woman unpacking beds from a cart.

"Please, have you seen a boy on a horse? He was wearing a scarlet shirt and a cowboy hat."

The woman stopped, with her hand on a brass bed knob that shone like a lump of gold in the sun.

"Why, yes," she answered. "I happened to notice him, because he spoke to my husband. He rode over to the west there. I don't think he meant to go much farther."

"Oh, thank you," replied Chris in relief. "And do you know the time, please?"

"Going on for five, I guess," said the woman and she turned back to her work.

So to the west went Dapple and the cart, with Chris and Curly and Kit.

"There he is!" shouted Curly after a while. "There's Elmer." There was Elmer—his cowboy hat pushed to the back of his head, his scarlet shirt streaked with dirt, his face grey with dust. He was in conversation with a man, and in the ground stood his stake, the stake with "Graham" carved near the top of it.

Eagerly, excitedly, Chris, Curly and Kit jumped down from the cart, and ran to him. But as they drew near, they stopped in their tracks, for Elmer's voice was loud and angry, and the man was ugly and threatening.

"It's my claim," the man was saying. "I staked it before you came anywhere near. There's my stake, by the corner stone."

"But I was here first," insisted Elmer. "I know I was."

"Look here, kid," said the man, "we've both staked the same claim, but I staked it first. If you clear off quickly, you may find a section somewhere else that hasn't been taken, or you may find someone willing to sell to you."

"Sell!" echoed Elmer bitterly. "What'll I use for money?"

"Well, you won't get anywhere by standing arguing with me. It's my claim, and I'll defend it, see?" He took a pistol from his belt, and directed it at Elmer. Whether he ever meant to shoot, or just to frighten Elmer, no one knew—for Chris, desperate with fear and anger and weariness, took a flying leap, and hurled herself upon him.

The man went down with the unexpected force of the attack, and the pistol rolled out of his hand. Curly and Kit began to cry at the tops of their voices. Elmer snatched the pistol. Chris stood irresolute, amazed at what she had done, and wondering fearfully what would happen next.

The man was on his feet again at once.

"Give me that pistol," he said.

"I won't!" cried Elmer, holding it behind his back. The man rushed at him, and tried to get hold of it. They both fell, then struggled together on the ground.

At that moment the wild and frightened cries of Curly and Kit brought help. Three men and a woman looked up from an adjoining claim, and hurried over to the rescue. One hastily took the pistol from Elmer's bruised hand, and another separated the two.

"What's the trouble?" they asked.

"This kid's stolen my claim," shouted the man.

Elmer was dusty and bruised and shaken, and so out of breath that he could speak only in gasps.

"It's my claim," he protested. "I've been on it for about two hours.—That's my stake—and this man suddenly appeared from those bushes, and, and—"

"And he tried to kill my brother," put in Chris.

"Well," said one of the men, whose name was Jock, "I saw this kid in the scarlet shirt ride up at three o'clock, and there was no sign of any rival then."

"There's my stake," the man shouted.

"And there's ours," said Chris.

The woman glanced at Jancy, lying stretched out on the grass, and then across at the man's horse, cropping a bush.

"Pity we can't ask the horses," she remarked.

"I guess they can tell us without being asked," said one of the other men. "The horse cropping the bush over there looks fresh enough. I should say he and his master have been all night in hiding on the Oklahoma lands."

"That's it," put in Jock—"breaking the law, cheating honest folk out of their rightful claims. Look at this horse" (pointing to Jancy). "He's still tired. He has run the race fairly."

The man saw that he was beaten. He muttered something about "kids making claims," strode off to his horse and rode away. Elmer and Chris breathed a sigh of relief.

"Where are your mother and father?" asked one of the men.

"Father has broken his leg, and mother is ill," explained Chris. "That's why we had to stake the claim ourselves."

"Well, I'm glad you've been lucky. You deserve to be," said Jock. "Where will you sleep tonight?" he added. He could see how tired they were.

"We have a tent," replied Elmer.

The men began to help him unload the cart, and pitch the tent. The woman walked away saying,

"Come and have supper with us tonight. I'll let you know when it's ready."

So a little later the children had supper, sitting round a camp fire with their kindly neighbours. Jancy and Dapple cropped the long, sweet grass close by, and the cart stood empty beside the tent. In the tent were the stores of food and water, the mattresses, blankets, pots and pans, and Mother's arm chair.

Daylight began to fade. In the distance an old man was digging a ditch, and already people were starting to build wooden shacks and houses of turf. Tents and covered wagons were scattered far and near. The sun touched the earth with pink and gold, till all the prairie glowed with the beauty of evening.

"Take a good look round," said Jock slowly to the children. "In a year or two, in a few months maybe, there'll be a busy town over there, and all this land will be yellow with waving corn as far as you can see. Then you'll remember tonight, and you'll be able to say, 'I knew this place when it was nothing but wild prairie. *I* was in the Run for Oklahoma.'"

"I'll remember that all right," said Elmer with a smile.

Kit was dozing in the woman's arms. Curly had been trying hard to keep awake, but he fell forward suddenly into Chris's lap.

"Curly doesn't care about history," remarked Jock. "He just wants his night's rest. I don't suppose he'll even remember the staking of the Graham family's claim."

"He's only five," said Chris, putting her arm round him and making him comfortable. "Look, Elmer. Look at the sunset."

Elmer looked. The sun spilled in a stream of red across the sky, and the prairie grass gleamed as gold as the corn that would one day cover the Oklahoma lands.

"It all depended on us," thought Elmer. "Well, we've managed all right."

The Story of Flying

There have always been children who have spread their arms wide, and run over the windy green hills of the world, hoping and hoping that their running might suddenly become flying. There have always been people who have gazed up at the birds skimming through the air, and have wished and wished that they might fly too. But for thousands and thousands of years, all the hoping and the wishing remained just hoping and wishing, and people flew only in their dreams and their daydreams.

There are many old stories about people who flew, and though at times they were half believed, *we* know that they were only legends.

A Greek legend tells of two men (Dædalus and Icarus) who were imprisoned on the Island of Crete far out at sea. In order to escape, they made themselves wings from birds' feathers, stuck together with wax. They flew well for a while, and Dædalus at last reached the mainland in safety, but Icarus was not so fortunate. He flew so high that the sun melted the wax. His wings came to pieces, and he fell into the sea and was drowned.

One of the first people to put his daydreams to some use was Leonardo da Vinci, who made tiny toys of very thin wax. He filled them with hot air, and they rose to the ceiling. He studied birds very carefully, and used his knowledge of their flight in making diagrams and notes about flying machines which might be made by man—machines with flapping wings of bamboo and linen. His notebooks contained many drawings and instructions on the subject of flight, and he is looked upon as the inventor of the helicopter and the parachute.

Nearly two hundred years later an Italian priest, named de Luna, made plans for a flying boat, which was to be guided by a sail, and kept up by four globes made of thin copper. The air was to be forced out of the globes in order to make them lighter than the air in which they were to float. De Luna described the flying boat, and drew pictures of it, but he didn't get as far as actually making it because he had a sudden clear and terrible vision. He saw how his flying boat might be used in warfare of the future—to fly over ships and cities, and drop balls of fire from the skies.

Another hundred years passed, and then things really began to happen. There were at that time two brothers named Montgolfier, who lived in France. They noticed that smoke from fires and chimneys always went upwards, and they made some experiments to see if smoke enclosed in a bag would still go upwards. They filled small paper bags with smoke from the kitchen fire, and found that the bags rose to the ceiling. Then they made bigger bags, and sent them up out of doors. Some of them rose to a great height. The Montgolfier brothers then decided to make a larger bag still, and send it up in public. This bag was made of silk, and buttoned together in sections in the shape of a ball. It was blue with patterns of gold upon it. It was lined with paper, and filled with smoke; and in the year 1783 it sailed into the air for everyone to see. It was the first hot-air balloon.

Shortly afterwards the brothers made another balloon in the same way, with a basket fixed below for the first passengers. A great fire was built below it, and the smoke gradually filled the balloon. Huge crowds had come to watch it, and they saw it rise silently into the air. No one knows what the passengers thought about the journey, for they were—a sheep, a cock and a duck. These animals stayed in the air for eight minutes, sailed two and a half kilometres on the breeze, and landed safely, none the worse for their adventure.

During the same year another man in France made a balloon, which he filled with gas called hydrogen. It floated some distance and started to descend over a field. People working on the land watched it in terror, wondering what kind of terrible creature it could be. As it landed, they rushed at it with their pitchforks, and attacked it wildly. As the pitchforks pierced the fabric, the hydrogen came out with a rush, and the balloon sank into a small heap of tattered cloth on the ground.

The people of France, and soon of other countries too, became very interested in balloons, and many ascents were made with human passengers. The difficulty of course was that balloons had to travel with the wind, and therefore could never set out for any special place. Sails and strange oars were tried, and suggestions were made that eagles should be harnessed, and trained to pull balloons through the air, as horses pulled carriages on land, but none of these ideas was successful.

The first man to cross the Channel in a balloon was a Frenchman named Blanchard. His wife became famous too, for many flights in balloons.

Ascents and experiments continued for a hundred

and fifty years and more, but during that time a more important idea was developed—the idea of gliding. Once more men turned their eyes towards birds. Several people drew plans for winged flying machines. They studied the effect of air and current upon small models which often seemed to work quite well.

About seventy years after the French brothers Montgolfier had sent up their first balloon, two small German brothers began to watch birds and butterflies, and to wonder just how they managed to sail so smoothly through the air. These boys—their name was Lilienthal—tried making wings and fixing them to their arms. The wings were not successful, but the boys never gave up hope, and at last, when they were grown up, they found and gave to the world the secret of gliding. Their glider was shaped rather like the wings of birds, and made of fabric stretched over a framework of willow twigs. There was a space in the middle, where the pilot was supported by pads under his arms. He would climb to the top of a small hill, run a little way to get a start, and then glide with the wind, his body and legs dangling below.

It took considerable practice, but the brothers made hundreds of successful glides, often gliding a hundred metres or more. The Lilienthal brothers proved that man could fly, if only for a few seconds, and many other people began to experiment in gliding.

The gliding of the Lilienthals gave new ideas to two American brothers whose name was Wright. In their childhood the Wright brothers had made tiny, flying models of paper and bamboo.

Now, thrilled by the story of the Lilienthals, they took up gliding. They studied wind and weather and machines. They built a glider of a different pattern, with one wing above the other. The pilot had to lie forward on the lower wing.

Although the gliders they made were successful, the Wright brothers were not satisfied. Gliders certainly kept afloat in the air, but without wind to drive them they were useless.

The brothers began to dream of a glider that would fly under its own power.

They worked hard for years and years, with many trials and failures, and at last they built a large machine, fitted with a petrol engine.

Then on a cold December day in the year 1903, they tried it. One of the brothers lay on the lower wing to pilot the machine, while the other stood on the ground, holding a watch to time the flight. There were only five people to watch their triumph, for a triumph it was. The machine flew. It was the first flying machine to be driven and controlled by man—the first real aeroplane.

From that time the building of aeroplanes improved so quickly in so many small but necessary details, that it is impossible to mention all the types of machines that were made, and all the stories of bravery and endurance in flight. The important milestones were the first Channel crossing, the first flight across the Atlantic, the first flight round the world.

Journeys that take weeks by land or sea can be completed in a few days by air. Journeys that used to take days can now be done in hours. There are speed records undreamed of in earlier days. There are jet-propelled planes that fly faster than sound.

Today there is always the hum of an engine or the flash of wings somewhere in the sky—for after centuries of dreaming, man has learned the secret of flight.

But the birds still skim and glide and turn above the trees, with the perfect balance they have always had—for they have known the secret since the world began.

Helen in the Dark

The air was filled with the sweet smell of honeysuckle, trailing over the front of the veranda, and sending little exploring tendrils creeping up towards the roof. Everywhere in the garden leaves were unfolding, buds were blossoming, and birds were singing their spring songs of delight.

It was a beautiful day in a beautiful part of America. Yet no one in the house seemed particularly happy—except perhaps the baby, lying in her cradle, and clutching at specks of sunshine with her small, curled-up fingers. From one of the rooms came the sound of crying and kicking. That was Helen. Helen was six years old. Something had made her angry, and she was having one of the fearful bursts of temper which the family dreaded. She battered at the wall with her fists, and kicked furiously with her feet, and no one could make her stop. She threw herself down on the floor, and kicked harder than ever. She cried and sobbed.

Father, walking up the path to Mother, asked wearily,

"What's the matter with her now?"

"I don't really know," Mother sighed.

"It's time someone drove to the station," said Father, looking at his watch. "Shall I go?"

"I'll go this time," replied Mother. "You've been so often these two days. Oh, I hope Miss Sullivan will arrive on the next train, and I hope she'll be able to help us with Helen. She's so naughty and difficult."

Mother stepped up into the carriage, and drove to the station. Father returned to the garden. Helen went on kicking and crying until she was worn out with the effort. Then she became quiet, rubbed away her tears, and clambered up into the window seat where she sat for several minutes.

Poor little Helen. No wonder she was angry so often. She was blind and deaf and dumb. She saw nothing of her own lovely garden. She heard none of the kind voices always near her. She understood scarcely anything that went on around her. And worst of all, she had no way of making *herself* understood. All the energy which should have been used for seeing, hearing and speaking was stored up inside her. No wonder she grew angry when she *couldn't* explain what she wanted to do. No wonder she used her energy for kicking, screaming and crying. It was like living in a dark prison, where no glimmer of light, and no murmur of sound ever came to bring happiness and understanding.

Sadly Helen sat in the window seat, tired out, though angry still and bitterly unhappy.

Meanwhile Mrs Keller, her mother, had arrived at the station and had met the lady she had been expecting, and even now she was bringing her back in the carriage.

"Oh, I'm so glad you've come," said Mrs Keller, holding the reins. "I'm *so* glad you've come."

"I'm glad too," replied Miss Sullivan. "I am looking forward to meeting your little girl, and trying to teach her." She looked at the country through which they were passing, and the beauty of it brought waves of happiness to her. Once, she too had been blind. So she knew what it was like to be always in darkness. But to be deaf as well, and not to be able to speak—that must be a thousand times worse.

"Tell me about Helen," she said.

Mrs Keller sighed.

"She was the loveliest baby you could imagine," she began, "and until she was one and a half, she could see and hear as well as anyone else. She had been walking for a few months, and was just learning to say a few words in a baby way, when she became very ill.

The doctor thought she would die, but one day the fever left her as suddenly as it had come. We were so thankful she was well again that for a day or two we didn't notice what the illness had done to her. It had left her blind and deaf—and of course dumb, for how could she learn to talk when she never heard a spoken word again? She's six now, and I'm afraid she's difficult and naughty, but it's hard to teach her the difference between right and wrong, and it's harder still to be cross with her. Look! We're nearly home."

Miss Sullivan gazed at the house just coming into view, and she trembled with excitement at the thought of seeing the little girl she had come to teach.

By this time Helen was on the veranda. Perhaps she felt the house shaking with the rumbling of the carriage wheels, and guessed a visitor was coming from the station. Suddenly she knew that people were on the veranda near her, and she spread her arms wide to find out who they were. She felt Mother and Father, and then someone strange. She stood uncertainly a moment. Then she felt the stranger lift her up and hold her tightly in loving arms.

Helen didn't know, and no one could tell her about it, but Miss Sullivan had come to open the doors of the world to her—and the doors were to be opened, not with the keys of eyes or ears or voices, but those of the fingers.

Helen might have been a pretty little girl for she had pink cheeks and fair curls, but there was something strange about her face. It had no expression upon it, and she scarcely ever smiled. There was no warm, alive look about her. She was healthy and strong, very strong indeed. If she wanted something badly, she would fight for hours if necessary until she obtained it. People nearly always let her have her own way—her parents, the servants, the children who came to play with her. They gave in to her partly because they did not want to rouse her temper, and partly because they were sorry for her. She wouldn't let anyone kiss her or hold her except her mother; and sometimes she even felt angry with her baby sister for being on Mother's lap when she wanted to sit there herself.

There were many things that puzzled the little deaf, blind Helen. Sometimes when she sat on Mother's lap, she put her fingers on Mother's face, and felt her lips moving. Why? Why did Mother make her lips go into different shapes so often? Helen tried moving her own lips, but nothing special seemed to happen when she did it.

Sometimes she found Father sitting in a chair holding a sheet of newspaper in front of his face. Why? Helen tried holding a sheet of newspaper in front of *her* face. She even put on Father's glasses, but nothing happened. There was some secret, some magic about newspaper and moving lips that she didn't understand. What was it? What was it that other people did that she couldn't do? What was it?

When Miss Sullivan unpacked her trunk next morning, she gave Helen a doll. Helen liked dolls. She felt the shape of its head and body and arms and legs. She pointed to herself and nodded her head, by which she meant,

"Is it for me?"

Then Miss Sullivan took Helen's hand, and spelled into it with her fingers, "d-o-l-l." She did it again, and tried to get Helen to copy her. After a while Helen spelled it with her fingers, "d-o-l-l," but she had no idea what she was doing, or what the feeling in her hand meant.

Every day Miss Sullivan taught her a few words. When she gave Helen milk to drink, she spelled "m-i-l-k" into her hand, and made her spell it back. When the dog walked by, and Helen felt his furry coat, Miss Sullivan spelled "d-o-g" into her hand. By the end of four weeks Helen could spell, with her fingers, twenty-one words. She must have thought it was a new game. Certainly she didn't understand it, or know any reason for doing it. She even tried to teach the dog to spell with his claws.

Then came a most wonderful day—a day that Helen and Miss Sullivan and Mother and Father remembered for ever. Miss Sullivan wanted to teach Helen the word for water, so she led her to the pump that stood in the garden, and held the little girl's hand under the flowing water. It was icy cold, and Helen shivered as she felt it splashing through her fingers. At the same time the teacher spelled "w-a-t-e-r" into the other hand. At that moment something awoke in Helen's brain. Her hands fell to her sides. She stood quite still in wonder and amazement. Suddenly she understood that everything had a name, and she understood the sense of the game she had been playing.

That cold, wet stuff was called "w-a-t-e-r." The fluffy thing that walked was called "d-o-g." The thing she dressed and undressed was called "d-o-l-l." Everything had a name, and the way to get anything she wanted was not to scream and cry and kick, but to spell the name of the thing into someone's hand!

An expression of joy crept into her face, making her look radiant and lovely. It was as if a beam of light had found its way into her dark prison. It was as if the beginning of a tune had broken the silence.

She spelled "water" into Miss Sullivan's hand several times. Then she pointed to the ground and wanted to know the name of that. On the way back to the house she was so excited that she touched nearly everything she passed, and wanted to know its name. So she learnt Mother, Father, teacher, baby, door, open, shut—one word after another, and in a few hours she could spell with her fingers thirty new words.

From that day a change came over Helen. The wild, difficult little girl became sweet and gentle. She danced from one thing to another, wanting its name. She rushed to Miss Sullivan again and again, kissing her for joy. She spelled into her mother's and father's hands, and they spelled into hers. She taught her little friends how to do it, so that she could "talk" to them as well. Her face changed too. It became eager and alive. She smiled and laughed so much that people around her were filled with happiness themselves because she was such a joyous child!

Soon she began to put words together and make sentences, rather in the way that a baby does. When she

wanted to take a doll to bed with her, she spelled out,
"Doll will sleep with girl."

When she wanted to rest, she spelled,

"Legs very tired. Legs cry much."

Now, a baby understands a great many words long before he uses them himself, and Miss Sullivan decided to let it be like that with Helen. So she took her for country walks, and for visits to friends, and all the time she spelled into her hand, describing the things she saw around her, and repeating the amusing things that people said. In this way Helen learnt more and more words, and became very interested in everything. Then, like all children, she asked many questions, and sometimes Miss Sullivan found them difficult to answer.

"Flies bite," spelled Helen. "Can flies know not to bite? What colour is think?"

By the end of seven weeks Helen could use a hundred words. By the end of eleven weeks she knew three hundred. By the end of fourteen weeks she knew four hundred.

Life now became full of interest for her. She went to a Christmas party. She stretched out her arms and felt the lower branches of the Christmas tree, laden with presents, and Miss Sullivan wrote in her hand, telling her about the gay decorations and the glittering lights.

She went to the circus. There she was allowed to feel the soft little lion cubs, and to shake hands with a big, black bear. She was lifted on to an elephant's back, and then lifted high in the air so that she could feel a giraffe's ears, and know how tall giraffes were. The clowns and the tightrope walkers let her feel their costumes, and she was allowed to keep her hand gently on a donkey while he did his tricks. What a lovely day it was!

Soon Helen learnt to read—not from ordinary books of course, but from the special books that are made for blind people. The written language of the blind is called braille, and instead of letters, it has dots raised up on the paper, so that blind people can feel them with their fingers.

Now that Helen was learning so much about the world around her, she began to realise that she was different from other children. She touched her eyes one summer day, and spelled,

"What do eyes do?"

"*My* eyes see things," answered Miss Sullivan.

Helen walked on for a few minutes, thinking deeply. Then she wrote in Miss Sullivan's hand,

"*My* eyes are sick."

"I see things with my eyes," spelled Miss Sullivan, "but you see things with your fingers, don't you?"

And in a way this was true, for Helen's fingers did the work of her eyes and her ears. She knew the beauty of a rosebud by the feel of its fragile petals. She knew how an insect looked when it flew, because sometimes when she touched a flower, she felt tiny wings beating against her hand. She put her hand in a pond, and felt little, slippery tadpoles swimming between her fingers. When she spelled something funny into Mother's hand, she put her fingers up quickly to Mother's face, and so she knew when Mother laughed. She held her dog, and felt him bark. She kept her hand on the piano when someone played, and so she enjoyed the rhythmic beat of the music.

She knew all her friends just by the touch of their hands, or the feel of their clothes. She even knew whether people were happy or sad—but no one could be sad for long when Helen was near. Everyone loved her. She was so merry and gay.

But there was one thing Helen longed to do. She wanted to speak, not only with her fingers, but with her mouth, like other children. She knew that she had a voice. It was just that she did not know how to use it, because she never heard anyone speak. She could laugh and cry. Why shouldn't she learn to speak—with her mouth? She opened her lips and began to make queer noises.

"No, Helen," said Miss Sullivan with her fingers. "The voice is very tender, and if you use it the wrong way, you may harm it."

"I want to talk with my mouth, like other children," spelled Helen.

"No, Helen dear, you can't learn to speak. It's too difficult for you."

"Blind girls speak with their mouths. How do blind girls learn?"

"Blind girls can hear voices and words. It's easy for them."

"Some deaf children learn to speak. How do deaf children learn?"

"Deaf children can watch people's lips. It's very hard for them, but they can learn."

"Perhaps I could learn too. I could feel your lips."

But Miss Sullivan shook her head, and made her

fingers say,

"No. I'm afraid you would become unhappy. You would try so hard, and then feel sad because you couldn't manage it."

But Helen kept on trying. She wandered about the house, making sounds which she called speaking, and putting her fingers on her lips and her throat to feel the movement. Oh, if she could *only* learn to speak—so that her little sister would understand her—so that the dog would come when she wanted him—so that Mother would know what she meant without watching fingers. Oh—if *only*—

When Mr and Mrs Keller saw how determined Helen was to learn, they sent her with Miss Sullivan to a special teacher of the deaf in a large town some miles away. So at last Helen began lessons in speech, and one day a little later she spoke her first real sentence,

"It is warm."

"It is warm. It is warm." She said it to trees and flowers and birds and animals. She spoke it with her lips like other people. The little blind and deaf girl was learning to talk.

She had to try again and again, and to practise hard. Of course she couldn't hear her own voice, but she learnt to know by the feeling in her throat whether she was getting the sounds right or not. She had to work and work.

She kept on trying and trying and trying, and practising, practising, practising, again and again and again.

At last came the happy day when Helen could speak well enough to leave the special teacher. She knew that she would have to go on practising perhaps all her life, but now she had made a start, Miss Sullivan could help her at home.

All the family went to meet Helen's train—Mother, Father and little sister.

"Here it is!" cried little sister.

"There's Helen!" said Father.

Helen and Miss Sullivan stepped down from the

train. Helen held out her arms to feel the people she loved so much.

"Mother," said Helen—and she said it with her lips. "Father—little sister!"

As she spoke, she put her fingers up to Mother's lips, to find out what she would say, but Mother's happiness was so great that she was silent. She could only hold Helen tightly in her arms, and listen to the sweetest sound she had ever heard—Helen speaking to her for the first time.

Even that is not the end of the story, but there is so much to tell that it cannot all be written here.

Nearly everyone in the world has heard of Helen Keller now—how she went to school and even to college, with Miss Sullivan beside her in the classroom,

Helen Keller and Annie Sullivan

Helen at her graduation from college in 1904

spelling the lessons into her hand—how she had question papers printed specially for her in braille—and how, with girls who could see and hear, she passed all the examinations, and took a degree at an American university.

Helen Keller was surely one of the most wonderful women in the world. Though she had been dumb, she learnt to speak, and though she was blind and deaf, she found the way to knowledge and understanding.

"Everything has its wonders," she once wrote, "even darkness and silence, and I learn, whatever state I may be in, therein to be content."

Stories of Phineas Barnum

Phineas Barnum was a showman. He lived in America in the days when there were no films, and few theatres or amusements. He gathered together curios and strange creatures from all parts of the world. He charged people an entrance fee, and made a great deal of money from his shows.

The Way Out

One day so many people swarmed into the building where the show was held that there was scarcely room to move.

"Don't let anyone else in for a while," said Barnum to the ticket seller. "We'll wait till some of these people go out again. It won't take them long to see everything."

So the ticket seller closed the gate, and huge crowds were kept waiting outside. Meanwhile the people inside the show wandered round, talking to each other, and looking at the animals and the curios. They were not at all in a hurry to leave. They looked at the same things over and over again. Some of them sat down and started taking out sandwiches.

"Might as well make a day of it," Barnum heard a woman say. That was all very well for those who were inside, but what about those who were still waiting outside? The crowds at the ticket office were getting larger every moment.

"I'll have to do something," thought Barnum. Just then he met one of his painters, and an idea came to him.

"Paint me a notice, please," he said. "I want these words in large letters—'To The Egress'. Do it as quickly as possible, will you?"

The painter found a piece of canvas, and very soon the notice was finished.

"To The Egress."

Barnum hung it up on a door at the back of the building, and it was soon seen by large groups of people who wandered that way.

"Oh, look!" they exclaimed. "To the Egress. Here's an animal we haven't seen." So through the door they went.

"What's an egress?" asked others. "Let's go and see, shall we?"

Barnum smiled. He seemed to be the only person who knew that egress was just another word for "way out" or "exit".

Gradually all the sightseers moved along that way. They flocked to the egress by the hundred, pushing and jostling each other through the door. Then they stared round in amazement as they found themselves, not before the cage of some wild animal—but out in a street at the back of the exhibition building!

Barnum meanwhile went to the ticket seller, and said with a laugh,

"Let the others in now."

And the waiting crowds put down their money, and swarmed happily into the show.

The Only Razor

Phineas Barnum's grandfather, in company with several men from the same village, once went by sailing ship to New York, from a port not far away. They left in the evening, and expected to arrive early the next morning, but unfortunately there was little wind, and the ship was forced to go very slowly. Soon the weather became so calm that not a ripple moved on the water, and not a breath of wind stirred in the sails. Days and nights passed, and New York was still some distance away.

Grandfather and his companions amused themselves as well as they could, and were glad that the ship carried food enough to feed them all.

Now no one on the ship had brought a razor (except Grandfather) so no one was able to shave. Day by day the hair on their faces grew longer and thicker, till everyone had a bushy growth of beard. Everyone laughed at everyone else, and Grandfather kept his razor hidden, and let his beard grow like the rest.

"Oh, for a nice, clean shave!" sighed one man.

"Who would have thought of bringing a razor for a voyage that should have taken one night?" said another.

"We'll all have to rush to a barber the minute we arrive."

Day by day the beards and bristles grew, and still there was no wind to blow the ship along. Soon Sunday, the seventh day, came, and by that time the smart business men were looking like wild creatures. But on that day the wind arose. At last the sail fluttered, and the ship continued her voyage.

"Good," said everyone.

"We'll be in New York just after lunchtime,"

promised the captain.

"Oh, dear!" wailed someone. "It's Sunday. There won't be a barber's shop open. How can we possibly walk through the streets of New York looking like this?"

They looked at each other in despair.

"Hasn't *anyone* a razor?" asked one.

"I have," said Grandfather. "I'll lend it to you in turns." He unlocked his case and brought out the razor. Everyone sighed with relief.

"There won't be time for us all to shave ourselves before we reach New York," said Grandfather, "and it wouldn't be fair for some of us to go ashore while the others are still waiting for their turns. So I suggest that each man shaves half his face, and passes the razor on to the next man. Then we'll pass the razor round again for the second half."

"All right. That's fair enough," agreed the men.

"As it's my razor, I'll start," said Grandfather. Carefully he shaved one side of his face, till it was smooth and clean. The men laughed loudly, for Grandfather looked very funny with a thick, bushy growth on one side of his face, and a beard on half his chin, and not a single hair on the other side. Grandfather's eyes twinkled, and he passed the razor to the next man.

At the end of an hour and a quarter, every man was half shaved. Each had one cheek and half of his chin clean and smooth, and the other cheek and the other half of his chin covered in bushy hair of black or brown or grey. Everyone roared with laughter because everyone else looked so funny.

"You'd better hurry," said the captain.

"All right," said Grandfather, taking the razor again. "Now for the other half!"

Carefully he shaved the other half of his face. He smiled with satisfaction. Now he looked smart and business-like once more.

The next man held his hand out eagerly for the razor.

"My turn," he said.

"Wait a minute," replied Grandfather. "It's getting blunt. I'll sharpen it a bit." He put one foot on the rail of the ship, and held the leather strop across his knee. He began to sharpen the razor.

"That'll be enough," said the next man impatiently.

"I may as well do it properly," answered Grandfather. He went on sharpening it.

Suddenly the razor flew from his hand. Over the rail it went—splash into the water!

There was a deathly hush. The half-shaved men looked at each other in horror, and the ship sailed silently into New York harbour.

"We'd better go to a hotel," suggested someone after a long silence. "We'll have to stay there till tomorrow, when the barbers' shops open."

As Grandfather was the only one who looked respectable, he led the way. The unfortunate men walked swiftly through the crowded streets, feeling very foolish and most unhappy. People whispered and smiled, and stopped to stare openly at the strange procession. Many of them followed, laughing and talking, until the poor men were hot with shame.

The hotel keeper greeted them with amazement, and then with hearty laughter which he could not hide.

"Why are you all half shaved?" he asked "Whatever has happened?"

"Nothing has happened," replied Grandfather, keeping back a smile. "This is the fashion in the place where these gentlemen live, and I think the people of New York are very rude indeed to stare and laugh because their own fashion is a little different."

It certainly was a joke for Grandfather, if not for his friends; and the nearest New York barber made quite a lot of money as soon as he opened his shop next morning.

Thought Reading

In one of Phineas Barnum's great exhibitions he had two men who called themselves "The Scotch Boys". One of them was blindfolded, and the other held up objects belonging to people in the audience, and asked questions about them.

"What is this?"

"A pencil," replied the blindfolded one.

"What colour is it?"

"Red."

The people in the crowd murmured,

"Isn't he clever?"

"What is this lady holding?" went on the first Scotch Boy.

"A handkerchief," said the blindfolded one.

"And this gentleman?"

"Money."

"How much is it?"

"A dollar."

The people in the crowd said,

"Isn't he wonderful?" and when they went home, they told their friends and families about it.

But the only wonderful thing about it really was the patience the Scotch Boys had shown in learning their secret code beforehand. Each question was different, and had one answer only. For instance, the Scotch Boy who asked the questions could take money from someone in the audience and ask the blindfolded one how much it was—but he could say it in all these different ways:

1. How much?
2. How much is this?
3. How much have we here?
4. Tell me how much?
5. Now how much?
6. Can you say how much?

According to their own arrangement, question number one could mean a dollar; number two, half a dollar; number three, quarter of a dollar; number four, two dollars; and so on.

In the same way, the question, "What is this?" would tell the blindfolded one the answer.

"What is this?"—would mean a pencil.

"Now what is this?"—would mean a pen.

"What have we here?"—would mean a watch.

"What am I holding?"—would mean a book.

You might like to work out a thought-reading system for yourself. Try it with colours.

"What colour is this?" (Red.)

It really depends on how many different ways you can find for asking the same question. If you can find enough, you might even become as clever as the Scotch Boys in Phineas Barnum's show.

Did You Know This about Whales?

Whales are the largest creatures that have ever existed. Although they live in the sea they are not fish, they are mammals. Whales are warm-blooded, have lungs and breathe through a blowhole. They bear their young alive and feed them on milk.

Scientists know from studying their skeletons that whales are descended from land animals. They have traces of bone that show that at one time they must have had four legs. Inside their flippers are small bones that look almost like hands.

The whale family, which includes dolphins and porpoises, is divided into two groups. The first group, the baleen whales, contains the largest whales. They have no teeth, but instead have flat plates of bony material called baleen in their mouths. The second group, the toothed whales, contains the large sperm whale as well as the smaller whales and the dolphins and porpoises.

Whales live in all the seas and oceans of the world. Many of them live in the coldest regions—the icy polar seas of the Arctic and Antarctic. Although they are so huge, baleen whales feed on small sea creatures called krill. They eat vast amounts of this by taking in great mouthfuls of water and then closing their jaws. This forces the water out of their mouths, leaving the krill behind.

The toothed whales are hunters and catch fish and other sea animals for food. The killer whale will eat almost anything that swims.

When winter comes, and the Arctic and Antarctic seas freeze over, this food supply is often cut off; so the whales migrate to warmer waters. They also bear their calves in tropical waters in the winter and return to the polar waters in the summer.

In the cold polar seas whales grow a very thick covering of fat to keep them warm. This is called blubber. For hundreds and hundreds of years whales have been hunted and killed for their thick blubber. It was heated to extract oil for making soap, paint, candles, cooking fat and many other products. Other parts of the whale were useful too. The skin was made into leather; the meat was used for animal food; the bones were ground down to make fertiliser; and the blood was used in glue.

Because whales were such useful animals, enormous numbers of them used to be hunted and harpooned. Tens of thousands used to be killed in one season alone. As a result, whales are now scarce and some kinds are almost extinct.

(*above*) A killer whale, showing its teeth

(*below*) A Southern Right whale, showing the plates of baleen in its mouth. On its head is a raised patch of rough, thickened skin called a "callosity". These are often several centimetres thick. Barnacles attach themselves to these callosities, making a very rough surface.

A Southern Right whale leaping out of the water. This is called "breaching".

A Blue whale

A White whale

A Humpback whale

We don't need whale products nowadays. We can get everything from other sources. People who care about these large and interesting creatures, and want to protect them, have been trying for a long time to control whaling. Some countries have banned the import of whale products and laws have been passed to protect some kinds of whale. But there are still a few countries with fleets of whaling ships—so whales are still in danger.

Radium

When Marie Curie was a little girl, there was something she liked better than any of her toys or even any of her books. It belonged to her father really, but she always thought of it as her greatest treasure.

It was a glass case, and in it her father kept things to do with science. There was a tiny pair of brass scales, with little round weights laid out in order of size. There were small bottles and glass tubes. There were little dishes of crystals, white and gleaming, blue and clear, green and shining.

Often in the evenings when her brother and her two sisters played and romped and laughed, Marie would walk away in the middle of a game and go and stand in front of the glass case. She would stare and stare silently at the strange and wonderful things inside it. She wanted to be a scientist herself when she grew up, but meanwhile there were a lot of other things to be learnt first.

Marie lived in Poland, where winter was always cold and white and beautiful. She dressed like the other schoolgirls, in a navy blue frock with a white collar. Her hair was curly, but it was pulled back in a tight plait so that it looked almost straight, except in one place where a tiny curl nearly always escaped.

She worked hard at school, and sometimes she and

her favourite sister, Bronya, talked about what they would do when they left.

"I want to be a scientist," insisted Marie. Her mind was quite made up about this. "I want to do something special that will help Poland."

"I want to be a doctor," said Bronya.

"We'll have to go to a university," said Marie.

"That will mean travelling to France," Bronya reminded her. "It's a long way, and will cost a lot. Father will never be able to afford the fees anyway."

"Never mind," said Marie. "We'll save up for ourselves."

So, even before they left school, the two girls began to earn a little money by giving lessons to children of the rich, and by doing other small, extra jobs in the town.

They worked and saved, and when they left school, they worked long hours and were able to save much more. The money seemed a lot to them, but it was very hard to save enough. They earned so little really, and the university fees and the journey to France would cost so much. Sometimes it seemed as if their dreams would never come true.

Then one day Marie had an idea. She said,

"Bronya, how much money have you saved?"

"Enough to pay for the journey and one year at the university," replied Bronya. "But it takes five years to like her thoughts, someone who loved science as she did. When most of Marie's examinations were over, she and Pierre hired a small shed in which to carry on their work. Sometimes they stayed there all day long and far into the night as well. To Marie and Pierre nothing in the world mattered as much as science.

One day they were working with a mineral called pitch-blende, when they discovered in it a new metal which gave out invisible rays. By measuring and using scientific instruments, they could tell that the new metal was there, although they couldn't actually see it. The rays it gave out were so strong that Marie and Pierre knew it would be very useful to doctors—if only they could find it and separate it. So they called it Radium, and began to search for it.

"As we know it's somewhere in pitch-blende," said Marie, "we'd better get more pitch-blende."

"Yes," murmured Pierre. "It's a pity it's so expensive."

Pitch-blende came from the mines of a distant country, but the two scientists were determined to get it. So they sent all their savings to pay for it. One day there was a knock at the door, and there outside was a cart loaded with full sacks.

"Oh!" cried Marie. "It's our pitch-blende."

They carried the sacks into the shed. With great excitement they opened one, and peered inside. The pitch-blende looked dull and brown and useless, but they knew that somewhere in it was Radium, one of the most precious metals in the world. If only they could find it! If only they could separate it!

They examined a little of the pitch-blende. They boiled it and stirred it for hours on end. They could feel the power of the invisible rays, but Radium itself they could not find. Then they took another pile of pitch-blende and started on that. The work went on for days and nights, for weeks and months, then a year, two years, three years. Every day they did the same kinds of things. It began to look as if Radium would never be found.

"Don't you think we'd better give up for a while?" said Pierre.

"Oh, no!" cried Marie.

"We can try again later when we have a better workroom," suggested Pierre.

"Oh, no!" said Marie again.

She had started to look for Radium, and she would search until she found it. So they continued, day after day, night after night, month after month, until another year had passed.

And then at last when they had almost given up hope—after a search lasting four years, Marie discovered the secret. She separated the Radium from the pitch-blende. She had found it! She could see it! She put it in a glass tube—just tiny little specks of it—but each one was worth thousands of pounds. Each one could be used by doctors to heal diseases for which there had been no cure. Each speck would relieve pain. Each speck would save lives.

In the dim shed the precious Radium glowed like a star in the night sky.

Marie Curie had done something to help Poland. She had done something to help the world!